David Roberts Dungan

Sabbath or Lord's day? Which?

David Roberts Dungan

Sabbath or Lord's day? Which?

ISBN/EAN: 9783743344952

Manufactured in Europe, USA, Canada, Australia, Japa

Cover: Foto ©ninafisch / pixelio.de

Manufactured and distributed by brebook publishing software (www.brebook.com)

David Roberts Dungan

Sabbath or Lord's day? Which?

Sabbath or Lord's Day?

WHICH?

By D. R. DUNGAN,
Author of "On the Rock."

CHRISTIAN PUBLISHING CO.,
St. Louis, Mo.

COPYRIGHT, 1855, BY
CHRISTIAN PUBLISHING CO.

Sabbath or Lord's Day?

WHICH?

CHAPTER I.

THE STATEMENT OF THE QUESTION.

The question is one of importance, as it concerns a matter of obedience to God. If God has required us to keep one day out of every seven, and if blessings and penalties depend upon our obedience or disobedience, it well becomes us to know whether we are in the way of blessing or cursing. All through the Old Testament, after the giving the law from Sinai, the Sabbath is made binding upon the people of Israel. Not only so, but it was enforced by very severe penalties. Like other features of that law, men must observe it or die. Found guilty of violating this law, the rebel must surely be put to death. Even picking up sticks on that holy day was a capital offence. No one attempts to deny these facts.

Again, it is just as evident that the seventh day was the Sabbath day as that there was a Sabbath day required to be kept by any one. The commandment was not to keep one day out of seven, but to keep the seventh day. If the Israelite had kept the first day of the week, with all the solemnity of the law, but not the seventh, he would have been regarded as a violator of the law, and punished accordingly. Indeed, he might have observed all the other six, but if he had not remembered the seventh to keep it holy, he would have been regarded as a transgressor of the law. This also is acknowledged by every one who has read the Scriptures on the subject.

If the Sabbath is now binding, are the penalties then belonging to the institution, yet to be inflicted upon the violator of the law? If not, when were these penalties removed, and by whom? If those penalties have been removed, are there any others come to take their place? And if there are other penalties, not found in the law of Moses, where can we find them? If there are any changes in the severity of the penalties, or in the rigor of the law, how can we assure ourselves of the fact?

If this law of the Sabbath is still binding, and yet without penalties for its violation, or blessings for its faithful observance, then it may be a matter of small moment to many persons, whether they keep it or not. If the blessing pronounced upon faithfulness to this requirement is eternal life, and the curse to be visited on the disobedient eternal death, where can we find the statement which will warrant our faith?

There is now a very earnest effort being made by Adventists and Seventh-Day Baptists to bring about a return to Sabbath-keeping, according to the law. If I have understood them correctly their positions are as follows:

1. The Sabbath was given at the creation of the world.
2. It was given to all men, and was to be observed during all time.
3. It was to be observed on the seventh day of the week.
4. The law of which it was a part has never been done away.

Now, beyond all question, if their theory is right, their practice can not be wrong. I understand the religious world generally to agree with their views concerning the giving of that law, as to form, time and extent. Indeed, I am not aware that either of the four positions taken by Sabbatarians is dissented from by the average religious teacher of to-day. Still, the practice is very distinct. The whole religious world, aside from the parties already named, keep the first day of the week instead of the seventh, which was required to be observed by the law.

Here is a manifest inconsistency, and no man can deny it. If God required us to keep the seventh day of the week, keeping the first will not be obeying that command. And it is vain to talk of keeping the spirit of a law when we deliberately violate its letter. It is impossible to be religiously right and scripturally wrong at the same time. If God commanded all men to keep the seventh day of the week, and has never changed or removed that law, then we must either keep the seventh day or violate the commandment of God. This is so self-evident that to elaborate or repeat it would indicate a want of confidence in my readers.

Some have been heard to say, however, that the Sabbath has been changed from the seventh to the first day of the week. But the Bible does not know anything of any such a change. No inspired man ever called the first day of the week the Sabbath. It was centuries after the last apostle was dead before men began to speak of keeping the Sabbath by observing the first day.

It will be said, however, that the Sabbath, as required of the Israelite, could not be observed in cold climates, and hence the rigor of the law must necessarily have been somewhat abated. But if any such necessity has existed, He who gave the law has surely known it quite as well as any of His creatures, and has therefore, somewhere in His word, removed the severities of the law, or, He has not intended it to be regarded in these cold climates. But if it was not intended for these northern countries then it was not meant to be universal. Hence all that may be legitimately argued from the fact of a needed change in the severities of the fourth command, is that it was not intended for persons living in cold climates. No one can change a law in any feature, except He who gave it. And if God had made any such a change, such amending enactment could be found somewhere in the Bible. But as no such enactment can be found, the law remains as it was.

I have heard a peculiar argument against the Sabbath to the effect that all men cannot observe the Sabbath at the same time; that when it is daylight on one side of the globe, it is night on the other. Hence, while one half of the world are keeping the Sabbath, the other part will be busily at work. They illustrate by starting two men around the world from the same place, but in opposite directions. With one the days get shorter, and with the other, they grow longer, so that the man going east has gained a day on his neighbor, at their next meeting; hence one will be keeping one day for Sabbath and the other will be keeping the next. And some ingenious person has made a reckoning, showing clearly enough, to himself, that we are really now keeping the seventh, and not the first day. All this seems to me very much like surrendering the question. These men say—without intending it—that the Sabbath keepers are right in their demands, and that it is necessary for us to find some way of excusing ourselves. Whatever difficulties there may be found in keeping the Sabbath in other countries or under other circumstances than could be found in Palestine, at the time it was intended for the Israelites, may show that it was not given to other peoples, but can have no effect to prove that the law has in any sense changed.

Again it is argued that Jesus taught the superiority, not only of man, but also of the beast, to the strict demands of the Sabbath. It is claimed that Jesus violated this law when occasion required, and justified himself in doing so on the ground that human want was of more importance than the letter of the law. But no man has yet been able to find a single instance in which Jesus violated any declaration of the law given by Moses. He could not do so after the statement we find in Matt. 5 : 17-19 :

"Think not that I am come to destroy the law, or the prophets : I am not come to destroy, but to fulfill. For verily I say unto you, Till heaven and earth pass, one jot or tittle shall in no wise pass from the law, till all be fulfilled. Whosoever therefore shall break one of these least commandments, and shall teach men so, he shall be called the least in the kingdom of heaven : but whosoever shall do and teach them, the same shall be called great in the kingdom of heaven."

No one could be the author of that language and then violate that law himself without gross inconsistency, such as would unfit him for a public teacher.

Christ neither violated the law nor winked at such conduct on the part of any one else. No case has yet been reported, and no such teaching can be found as coming from Him.

Sabbatarians are claiming, and with some show of reason, that a large majority of the Protestant clergy believe just as they do respecting the sanctity of the Sabbath, and that, if their popularity and salaries were not endangered, would advocate the keeping of the seventh day just as they do. They conclude this from their admissions, as before stated, which legitimately bind them to the law of the Sabbath. They further claim, too that the devotion of the Christian world to the first day of the week, is a superstition, which has no higher origin than the edict of a heathen king.

Now to my mind, the question resolves itself into this: Are we now under the law of which the Sabbath was a part, or is the Sabbath now binding on Christians? For certain it is, if we are to keep the Sabbath, then we are bound to observe the seventh day of the week.

No matter how the law was changed, unless Jehovah changed it, if it is yet binding, it is our place to keep it to the end of life, unless sooner released from its obligations by Him who gave it.

CHAPTER II.

REASONS FOR KEEPING THE SABBATH EXAMINED UPON THE HYPOTHESIS OF A PRE-MOSAIC REQUIREMENT.

I. The first reason usually assigned for keeping the Sabbath is that it was given at creation, to all men and for all time.

This position is called in question. If we can have no law respecting the *Sabbath* without the use of that word, then there was no command from Jehovah to any man to observe the Sabbath for at least 2,500 years after the world was framed. In Exodus 16:23 is the first occurrence of the word in the English Scriptures. Nor is there any text which would contain that word if properly translated. Just how a law was in existence requiring men to observe the seventh day of the week, and yet no mention made of the fact in the Bible, will never be solved in the minds of those who are disposed to think for themselves.

But some one answers, We find Cain and Abel offering sacrifice, and yet no mention made of the fact that God had required such service at their hands. Not only so, but Paul says that Abel offered by faith. And, as we know that faith is the belief of testimony, it therefore follows that commands are sometimes enacted when there is no notice given of the fact.

This, however, is a long ways from the case in hand. Here we find sacrifice. Though we have no mention made of the original command, we do have mention made of the practice. But there is no mention made of command or practice respecting the Sabbath for twenty-five centuries.

But it is said that God not only rested on the seventh day, but he sanctified it in commemoration of that fact. Hence it was set apart to a holy or a sacred use, and as this was at the beginning, the law was known from that time and observed by all who feared the Lord.

Two things are taken for granted here which are not granted. First, it is presumed that "*sanctified*," when said of the seventh day, means, necessarily, set apart to be observed by men as a day of worship; and second, that it was thus set apart at the creation of the world. But neither of these is by any means certain. "Sanctified" might refer to a holy joy in the mind of God; or it might indicate that God would mark the time, and in the ages to come require his people to abstain from labor on that day. Hence the language cannot mean anything absolutely which will be of any service to the cause for which it is used.

Nor is this all. The deductions from the supposed existence of the law of the Sabbath are by no means legitimate. For instance, if the law had been given at the creation it would not follow that all men were expected to obey it for all time. We are sure, from the reference to sacrifice, that an offering for sin was required, and that it was a sacrifice of blood, but these services are not therefore required of all men and for all time. When the seventh day was sanctified is not indicated in the language referred to. I will quote Gen. 2: 2, 3:

"And on the seventh day God ended his work which he had made; and he rested on the seventh day from all the work which he had made. And God blessed the seventh day, and sanctified it: because that in it he had rested from all his work which he had created and made."

Now it was not the first seventh day in which the sanctification took place, for he sanctified the day *because that in it he had rested*. The day was not wholly given to silence and inactivity; that is not the meaning. The thought is that he discontinued the creative or formative work on that day.

The following sensible treatment of the subject is found in Smith's Bible Dictionary, Am. Ed.; Vol. iv., page 2763:

"We have hitherto viewed the Sabbath merely as a Mosaic ordinance. It remains to ask whether there be indications of its having been previously known and observed; and, secondly, whether it have an universal scope and authority over all men.

"The former of these questions is usually approached with a feeling of its being connected with the latter, and, perhaps, therefore, with a bias in favor of the view which the questioner thinks will support his opinion of the latter. It seems, however, to us, that we may dismiss any anxiety as to the results we may arrive at concerning it. No doubt, if we see strong reason for thinking that the Sabbath had a pre-Mosaic existence, we see something in it that has more than a Mosaic character and scope. But it might have had such without an universal authority, unless we are prepared to ascribe that to the prohibition of eating blood or things strangled. And again, it might have originated in the law of Moses, and yet possess an universal scope, and an authority over all men, and through all time. Whichever way, therefore, the second of our questions is to be determined, we may easily approach the first without anxiety.

"The first and chief argument of those who maintain that the Sabbath was known before Moses, is the reference to it in Gen. 2:2, 3. This is considered to represent it as coeval with man, being instituted at the creation, or, at least, as Lightfoot views the matter, immediately upon the fall. This latter opinion is so entirely without rational ground of any kind that we may dismiss it at once. We have no materials for ascertaining or even conjecturing, which was put forth first, the record of the creation, or the Fourth Commandment. If the latter, then the reference to the Sabbath in the former, is abundantly natural. Had, indeed, the Hebrew tongue, the variety of preterite tenses of the Greek, the words in Genesis might require careful consideration in that regard; but as the case is, no light can be had from grammar; and on the supposition of these being written after the Fourth Commandment, their absence, or that of any equivalent to them, would be really marvelous."

Nearly all able critics are of the opinion that the whole of Genesis was written after the law had been given at Sinai. Hence, as Moses had learned that the Fourth Commandment was to keep in memory the creation of the world, the most natural thing would be for him to mention the sanctification of that day in connection with the account of the creation. This has been the manner of historians and biographists in all time. It is in this way that we speak of General Washington when he was a boy. And yet no man would understand us to say that he was a general at that tender age. As our learned author has indicated, there are no rules of grammar which require us to regard the time of that sanctification as having occurred previous to the giving of the law on Mt. Sinai, and as it is most in accord with all the facts known to us, to regard it as never having been mentioned before that event, it is safer to say that Moses referred to the sanctification of the Sabbath, as having taken place when the law was given at Sinai. This will account for the fact that no mention is made of any law of that nature during all these centuries.

In appropriating this text the friends of the Sabbath have to assume every essential feature of the argument:

1. They assume that Gen. 2:2, 3, describes an event which took place at the foundation of the world.

2. They assume in the second place, that "blessed and sanctified" require that man should observe that day as a day of rest, without any mention being made of the fact.

3. They assume in the third place, that if the law had been given at that time, it would therefore be binding upon all men for all time.

These are the very essentials, in the whole matter, and yet they are assumed; not one of them can be sustained.

It has sometimes been argued that Gen. 4:3, presents the idea of a pre-Mosaic Sabbath: "And in process of time" they render, "And in the end of days," which, they tell us, shows that they had knowledge of some artificial measurement of time, most likely the Sabbath.

This comes from too fruitful an imagination. The language does not indicate any artificial measurement of time, nor any division of time whatever. It is equal to saying that it occurred in the history of this family, etc. And if there was any division of time in the language, it would be more easily interpreted of the new moon, or of some measurement of time which we know to have been before the people. But the seizure of this and many similar passages of Scripture, only to force them into some sort of support of their theory, contrary to all probability and even possibility of meaning, only shows how far mere speculators will go in search of support for a favorite dogma.

Again we are told that this arbitrary division of time is to be seen in the seven days of Noah, and also in the week which Jacob fulfilled for Rachel (Gen. 29:27). While these things would accord well with the idea of a pre-Mosaic Sabbath, yet the existence of such an institution is not a necessary inference therefrom. If they could be accounted for in no other way, then we would give them a prominent place in the consideration of the subject. But such is not the case. Seven days is a natural division of the moon, by which we know that the ancients measured the year. And yet, for all that, the third day is of more frequent occurrence in Genesis than the seventh. It is not a natural division of time, nor does any one claim it to be sacred. And yet, the word week, in Gen. 29:27, has most probable reference to seven years, during which Jacob should continue his toils with Laban. It must be conceded that the word week everywhere else in the Old Testament has the meaning of seven years. Hence, when we come to look at this argument, there seems to be nothing in it.

The Sabbath must be found in some way, hence the ancient cities are put under tribute to the cause. Mr. Smith finds in Nineveh, (1869) the fifth of the Assyrian tablets, and also a religious calendar, in that ancient city. Here are evidences that the people knew of the Sabbath, and probably kept it. This, too, is supposed to have been written before the law of Moses was given on Mt. Sinai. Hence that people had carried down with them this religious requirement. But when we find the name of Merodach in this, we are quite sure of the later origin of this production. Certain, it is, that Solomon largely influ-

enced the nations of the east long before these tablets were probably written. And still further, it will be seen in these, that the service of the New Moons, and the feast days of the Jews stand in the same relation to time that the Sabbath does:
"*Every month without fail he made holy assembly days.*" And the whole of this tablet shows the common Jewish origin, with the after glosses of heathenism.

I have no need to say to any one who reads history that all reckoning upon dates, which claim to have been given, among the heathen nations before the seventh century, B. C., is exceedingly doubtful as to its correctness. Hence, since we know that these writings give certain evidence of their Jewish origin, nothing more need to be said of them.

A very strange argument, and yet a very common one, is that the form of the law of the Sabbath in the Decalogue is proof that it was an old institution. They say that as it there occurs, it has all the form of a requirement already known. But who does not know that the Sabbath was given a month before that? In Exodus 16 : 23, the word occurs for the first time in the Bible. But this was a month before the law was given at Mt. Sinai. If it could be said that the requirement to keep the Sabbath as it is found in Ex. 16 : 23 indicates that it was an old institution and well understood by the people, then there would be some argument in it. Even then, however, it would only be suggestive.

Ex. 16 : 22, 23 : "And it came to pass, that on the sixth day they gathered twice as much bread, two omers for one man; and all the rulers of the congregation came and told Moses. And he said unto them, This is that which the Lord hath said. To-morrow is the rest of the holy Sabbath unto the Lord; bake that which ye will bake to-day, and seethe that ye will seethe; and that which remaineth over lay up for you to be kept until the morning."

1. They are not reminded to renew their faithfulness in keeping an ordinance which they had previously known, but had, on some account, neglected.

2. But the institution is given in the form in which a new commandment is presented.

3. There is no account in their history that they had ever

kept it or known anything about it.

4. Every ruler seemed perfectly surprised that two portions of *manna* was given on the sixth day, and could not imagine why it should be so. If they had ever known anything about the Sabbath day before this, their ignorance and astonishment is perfectly unaccountable.

If we had found that the law of the Sabbath was given at the creation, it would not follow that all peoples are to observe it, for all time. Hence, in every way, the argument for a pre-Mosaic Sabbath, must be regarded as a complete failure.

CHAPTER III.

TO WHOM WAS THE LAW OF THE SABBATH GIVEN?

It is maintained that the Sabbath was given to all men, and was, therefore, intended to be a universal law. Of course the purpose of this argument is to find that the removal of the law given at Mt. Sinai can have nothing to do with the cessation of the Sabbath.

1. The first proof of the correctness of this position usually relied upon, is the numerical argument. A careful gleaning of the whole of the Scriptures is made and the number of times which the Sabbath is commanded, in one way or another, is stated. This is done to show the importance of the institution in the mind of the Author.

Surely this is a work of gratuity. If we could so far forget our logic as to imagine the possibility of maintaining any proposition in this way, we could easily find that almost every requirement of the Old Testament was intended for all men. Sacrifices, circumcision, new moons, sabbatical years, and almost the entire law has been required with equal emphasis. No one doubts that the Sabbath was binding on the people to whom it was given, and that it was to continue in force till it should be taken out of the way by the same authority which gave it.

2. But the great argument is derived from the statement of the Master: "The Sabbath was made for man, and not man for the Sabbath." Mark 2: 27. They repeat this very frequently, with very telling effect, at least on themselves.

And yet everything that was said of the Sabbath in this respect could have been said with equal propriety concerning every other Old Testament requirement. Every decree that God ever gave to the race, or any portion of it, was given to man, or made for man. But there is nothing in it to show that it was intended for all men. This is a rule in hermeneutics, agreed to by all who have really studied that science: *Nothing should ever be applied to any subject not before the mind of the author at the time of writing or speaking.* Indeed, the first thing that the exegete has to do in beginning his work, is to determine the purpose of the author, so that in the work of interpretation he may never go beyond that purpose in his exegesis.

Now with that rule before us, let us turn and see if Jesus was intending to say anything respecting the extensiveness of that institution. The question was, had his disciples violated that commandment? If we know the law in the matter, we know they had not. And as for their traditions, Jesus cared nothing. But while he and his disciples were free from transgressions of the law, *they* were not. *They* had violated that commandment, and excused others in doing the same. *They* had done so, too, when they had regarded it necessary to sustain life, or even to remove suffering. And yet upon such a basis as that, no law should be violated. One who was the Lord of the Sabbath might do so, for he would be unerring in his opinion of the necessity of the case. Hence he adds: "The Son of man is Lord also of the Sabbath." The argument, then, of Jesus stands: (1) My disciples have violated no law. See Matt. 12: 7. (2) You agree that human life is more than keeping the Sabbath, and if there is therefore ever a conflict between the two, the Sabbath will have to give way; and (3) I am the Lord of the Sabbath, and can therefore dispose of it as I please. Hence it will appear to every careful reader that in making Mark 2: 27 testify on the subject of the extent of the Sabbath, they have done violence to one of the most fundamental rules of interpretation; that they have insisted on a meaning that was not in any way before the mind of the Lord when the language was employed.

It now seems proper that I should state some reasons for denying the proposition. This I must do very briefly:

1. The Scriptures directly state that they were only given to ancient Israel. If this be true, the question ought to end. For if He who gave the Sabbath says it was only intended for the descendants of Jacob, no true believer will dare affirm the proposition which we now oppose.

Exodus 34:27: "And the Lord said unto Moses, write thou these words: for after the tenor of these words I have commanded a covenant with thee and with Israel."

No man, not even Adventists, deny that this covenant commanded, contained the Sabbath. Hence this law was given to Moses and the people of Israel. If this law belonged to others, what emphasis could have been placed on its being the property of Moses and that people?

Exodus 31:13, 16, 17: "Speak thou also unto the children of Israel, saying, Verily my Sabbaths ye shall keep: for it is a sign between me and you throughout your generations; that ye may know that I am the Lord that doth sanctify you." * * * * "Wherefore the children of Israel shall keep the Sabbath, to observe the Sabbath throughout their generations, for a perpetual covenant. It is a sign between me and the children of Israel forever: for in six days the Lord made heaven and earth, and on the seventh day he rested, and was refreshed."

Now whatever was a sign between God and his people was not equally intended for other people. God gave to Abraham and his seed the sign of circumcision. But if that mark had been put upon all other peoples, it would not have been a sign between God and the seed of Abraham. So with the law of the Sabbath, it could not have been a sign between God and that people if it had been given to others as well as to them. Hence, its being a sign is certain proof that it was not intended for any other nation.

Deuteronomy 4:8: "And what nation is there so great, that hath statutes and judgments so righteous as all this law which I set before you this day?"

This question can only be answered in the negative: "No

nation." It was intended to affirm that no nation was in possession of this law. With this statement men ought to be satisfied, so that when God says *no other nation possesses this law* the whole question should be dropped.

Deuteronomy 5:3: "The Lord made not this covenant with our fathers, but with us, even us, who are all of us here alive this day."

Now when God is said to have made that covenant with that people only, and not even with their fathers, it must be a strange form of faith that will contradict him by saying that he did make it with their fathers, and not only with them, but with all men and for all time. But some one may say that this covenant here spoken of, did not contain the Sabbath. This, however, is not correct. Read right along and see what the covenant was that was only given to them and not even to their fathers.

Coming to verse fifteen, we read: "And remember that thou wast a servant in the land of Egypt, and that the Lord thy God brought thee out thence through a mighty hand and by a stretched-out arm: therefore the Lord thy God commanded thee to keep the Sabbath day."

This not only shows that the Sabbath was not given to others but why it was given to the Israelites.

2. A second reason for believing that God only intended the Sabbath for the descendants of Jacob, is that it is never spoken of as in any way connected with any duty which He required of the Gentiles. They are never reproved for not having kept it. And yet it is certain that they never kept it.

He reproved the Jews for the want of faithfulness to that commandment; why not condemn the Gentiles for like negligence? He reproved them for their many sins; he judged them for their wickedness and maltreatment of Israel; for their idolatry; for their adultery and sodomy; for their want of natural affection. Nay more, He shows clearly the ground of their responsibility. But never does He reprove them for not observing the Sabbath. Now, upon the hypothesis that this law was given to them, these things are inexplicable.

3. The Sabbath could not be kept by those who live in cold climates. This will be seen in the nature of the institution.

(a) *No work should be done.*

Exodus 20:10: "But the seventh day is the Sabbath of the Lord thy God: in it thou shalt not do any work, thou, nor thy son, nor thy daughter, thy manservant, nor thy maidservant, nor thy cattle, nor thy stranger that is within thy gates." See Deut. 5:14.

(b) *They were to abide in their places.*

Exodus 16:29: "See, for that the Lord hath given you the Sabbath, therefore he giveth you on the sixth day the bread of two days: abide ye every man in his place, let no man go out of his place on the seventh day."

(c) *They must not even kindle a fire on the Sabbath.*

Exodus 35:3: "Ye shall kindle no fire throughout your habitation upon the Sabbath day."

(d) *The penalty for violating the law of the Sabbath was death.*

Exodus 31:14, 15: "Ye shall keep the Sabbath therefore; for it is holy unto you. Every one that defileth it shall surely be put to death: for whosoever doeth any work therein, that soul shall be cut off from among his people. Six days may work be done; but in the seventh is the Sabbath of rest, holy to the Lord: whosoever doeth any work in the Sabbath day, he shall surely be put to death."

Exodus 35:2: "Six days shall work be done, but on the seventh day there shall be to you a holy day, a Sabbath of rest to the Lord: whosoever doeth any work therein shall be put to death."

Numbers 15:32-36: "And while the children of Israel were in the wilderness, they found a man that gathered sticks on the Sabbath day. And they that found him gathering sticks brought him unto Moses and Aaron, and unto all the congregation. And they put him in ward because it was not declared what should be done to him. And the Lord said unto Moses: The man shall be surely put to death: all the congregation shall stone him with stones without the camp. And all the congregation brought him without the camp and stoned him with stones, and he died; as the Lord commanded Moses."

No one claims that such a law could be observed in this climate, say nothing of the Laplands, or the great area of northern countries. Hence, we are compelled to say that the law was not intended for any but those living in a land where the people could keep the law as it was given, or that its rigor has since then been abated, and that, too, by the same authority that gave it being.

Has the law been abated in its rigor, and yet left standing? Here the Bible is silent. It is commonly said that the law of the Sabbath now stands, but the penalty has been changed or taken away. But of all this, the Bible knows no more than it does of pilgrimages to Mecca. Jesus taught that not one jot or tittle of the law should in any wise pass till all should be fulfilled. Hence, the only way for these penalties to disappear can be found in the removal of the law as a whole. The penalties stand or fall with the law itself.

From all this, it is just as evident as it can be, that the law was given to the Israelites and to them alone. They were in a land where it might be observed. And they were expected to remain there. So far we are warranted in saying:

1. There is no account of the law having been given to any other people than the descendants of Jacob.

2. It is plainly stated that it was not even given to their fathers. Hence, that it was given alone to those who came out of Egypt, and to their children forever throughout their generations.

3. No Gentiles could be held responsible for a law that was never given to them. This accounts for the fact that they were never reproved for having disobeyed the law of the Sabbath.

4. The penalties of the law could only be removed by the authority which enacted them. God gave them, and he alone could remove them. Hence, as long as the law remained, even picking up sticks on the Sabbath must be punished with death.

It is left for us to see in the further discussion of the subject, how the penalties of that law were removed by the law being taken out of the way and nailed to the cross of Christ.

CHAPTER IV.

WAS THE LAW OF THE SABBATH PERPETUATED IN CHRIST?

No one doubts that the Jews were commanded to keep the seventh day of the week. But we have not found that any one else was required to observe that day. But God has designed his people to serve him. Has he directed them to continue to keep this law? If so, the whole question is at an end. No matter when that law was given, if its Giver intended it to be a continuous institution, then, beyond all controversy, it remains an eternal fixture. Those who demand that we should keep the Sabbath present several arguments on this point, and it is our duty to hear them. It will do no one any good to be mistaken in any matter like this. And it is certain if they who keep the Sabbath are right, most other persons are wrong.

1. It is claimed that the ten commandments are the moral code. And as the Sabbath is a part of the decalogue, it was therefore a moral commandment, or a part of the moral law.

It should be noticed here that our friends have to employ distinctions which are never found in the Bible. No inspired man ever called the ten commandments a moral law. The reason that men now so denominate it is that their theory cannot be sustained by simply using Scriptural terms. It is not clear to me that they have any definite idea of the meaning of the word moral. They seem to mean by the use of that term, anything which is right and pure. But in that sense, every feature of the law given by Moses was moral. Neither impurity nor injustice attaches to anything which God ever commanded men to do. And if such were the meaning of the word, there could be no reason for applying the term to one portion of the law, more than another. Webster's definition of the word is:

"Relating to duty or obligation; pertaining to those intentions and actions of which right and wrong, virtue and vice, are predicated, or to the rules by which such intentions and actions ought to be directed; relating to the practice, manners, or conduct of men as social beings in relation to each other, as respects right and wrong, so far as they are properly subject to rules."

This shows that the word moral refers to man's duty toward his fellow; that all its demands spring out of the relation which men sustain toward each other. Hence moral, is that which is right in the nature of things, in this respect, for justice between man and man can never change. But the Sabbath has no feature of the moral thought in it. It is not right in the nature of things to keep the seventh day any more than to observe the first, second, third, or any other day of the week. Nor does it regulate any duty of man toward his fellow, more than any feature of judicial or ritual procedure. It was right only because God required it. It was right just to the extent that he commanded it, and beyond that limit, there is no more authority for it, than for any of the mummeries and rites of the apostasy. It was given to Israel as a test by which God should prove them, whether they would keep his commandments or not. There are six moral enactments in the Decalogue, but the Sabbath is not one of them.

2. *It is claimed that we have the example of Christ and the apostles for keeping the Sabbath.*

Very certainly Christ and the disciples kept the Sabbath during the time that it was binding upon the people of Israel. Christ did not come to destroy the law but to fulfill it. This, however, was not truer of the Sabbath or the ten commandments than of any other portion of the law. Every "*jot and tittle*" of it was regarded as sacred by him. If this proves that the Sabbath is now binding, it proves that all of the law is binding, for he treated it all alike. Hence we know that the argument proves nothing. What was sacred during the life of Christ was done away in his death.

We find the apostles meeting in the synagogues on the Sabbath day. But that they observed it as a sacred day is no where stated. Adventists now meet on the first day of the week, not because they regard the day as a sacred day, but because they can have an audience to hear them on that day. For the same reason the apostles met in the synagogues on the Sabbath. Paul went a thousand miles to attend a Pentecost. But that does not bind that feast upon Christians. James reveals the fact that many believers were yet zealous in keeping the law of Moses. Does that fact make those services binding upon us, when we are told by inspiration that we are freed from the law by the body of Christ? Suppose that we shall find Christians who had been Jews were slow to learn that they were not under law, but under grace, will that bind the law upon us? Paul took and circumcised Timothy, because of the Jews which were in those quarters; will that make it necessary for us to be circumcised? It took a number of years before even the apostles knew that the Gentiles were to have the gospel preached to them. Will that in any way interfere with our authority to carry to them the word of life? The Holy Spirit was given to those men to guide them into all truth. But all needed knowledge did not come in a day. It was years in being given and in being established with signs following. And yet, even though the minds of disciples had to open gradually to the whole truth, there is no recorded instance of their meeting on the Sabbath after the day of Pentecost. There were Judaizers who taught that they must keep the law, but they never had any considerable following. And when we come to a completed revelation we learn that we are not under the law in any respect whatever. That while the law had served a valuable purpose as a school-master to bring us to Christ that we might be justified by faith, yet, faith having come, we are no longer under the school-master.

3. *But it is claimed that Jesus bound upon the disciples this institution.*

If this is true, then there is an end of all controversy respecting the matter. Where and when did he do this? Show this, and we will keep the seventh day, not because it is of the Decalogue, but because it is of Christ. We must have the statement of Christ however. Where is it? They say that it is to be found in Matt. 24:20. They were to pray that their flight should not be in the winter, nor on the Sabbath day; and as this referred to the destruction of Jerusalem, it would be about forty years after the death of Christ; hence he makes keeping the Sabbath a matter of prayer, forty years after the inauguration of his church.

As much reliance is placed upon this passage, I will quote it in full. Matt. 24:17-21: " Let him which is on the house-top not come down to take anything out of his house; neither let him that is in the field return back to take his clothes. And woe unto them that are with child, and to them that give suck in those days. But pray ye that your flight be not in the winter, neither on the Sabbath day: *for then shall be great tribulation, such as was not from the beginning of the world to this time, no, nor ever shall be."*

Why this is ever quoted by Adventists to show that the Sabbath would be sacred in the year seventy is not easily seen. As they argue that all penalties are removed in case of absolute necessity, there would be nothing wrong in their fleeing on that day. And as for any tradition concerning a Sabbath day's journey, they do not suppose that Christ ever attached any importance to it. Since, then, there would be no wrong in fleeing on the Sabbath day, if necessity should require it, there would be nothing in it that would, in any way, interfere with their flight out of Jerusalem. Hence they have already destroyed their argument on this Scripture.

There were a number of things which they were to avoid. (1) Coming down from the housetop to take anything out of the house. (2) Must not return from the field to take his clothes. (3) Woe unto them that are with child; (4) and to them that give suck. (5) Pray that your flight be not in the winter; (6) Nor on the Sabbath day. Would it be religiously or morally wrong to do any one of these things? The Adventist finds no sin in anything but fleeing on the Sabbath. He accounts for all the other inhibitions on the ground of inconvenience, or necessity. It is only the Sabbath that was surrounded by religious authority. There was just as much prohibition on fleeing in the winter as on the Sabbath day. But while, to them, it proves that the Sabbath would be regarded as sacred, it does not have that meaning concerning the winter. This shows that they can find in the passage just what they wish to find. It means inconvenience in five cases out of the six, but in the sixth it must mean the sacredness of the day. Certainly Jesus knew it would be difficult for them to flee on the Sabbath day. The customs and rules of the people, whatever might be in the minds of the disciples respecting it, would make it almost impossible for them so escape from the doomed city on that day. Their fellow Jews would suspect them and apprehend them as traitors.

Hence, while this command of the Savior cannot be accounted for upon the hypothesis of the sacredness of the day, it is easily understood in the light of the others, convenience : and necessity.

4. *Paul is said to bind upon them this law in his letter to the saints in Rome.* See Rom. 3 : 31 : "Do we then make void the law through faith ? God forbid : yea, we establish the law."

There are two questions to be settled in determining the meaning of this passage. (1) What is meant by the word law? and (2) what is meant by "we establish the law" ?

Of course Adventists understand the term law here to refer to the ten commandments, to the exclusion of all the rest. For, with them, it will not do to have the rest of the law bound upon Christians. Though nothing has been said about the Decalogue in the connection, yet it must have that meaning, forsooth, *it must.*

Those who will be at the pains of reading this letter from the beginning up to this text will find that Paul was trying to convince them that the gospel was the only power by which men could be saved. To do this he had shown (1) that all men were lost, and therefore were in need of salvation. (2) That they could not be saved by the law. (3) But that they could be saved through the gospel without the deeds of the law. Now what law is established in this way ? Let me read the 28th, 29th and 30th verses: "Therefore we conclude that a man is justified by faith without the deeds of the law. Is he the God of the Jews only ? Is he not also the God of the Gentiles ? Yes, of the Gentiles also. Seeing it is one God which shall justify the circumcision by faith, and the uncircumcision through faith."

Now it will be seen by every reader that the same law that was established by the gospel, was that law by which they could not be saved ; *without the deeds of which they might be saved.*

(2) But now the question recurs : In what sense was that law established ? Does Paul mean to say that a law by which no man could be saved, and that without performing its deeds they might be saved, had been bound upon them as a rule of life ? Such a thought is perfectly unreasonable. You know that Paul never said any thing of the kind. Hence, in establishing this law he has not the remotest idea of binding it upon

them as a rule of life. But what does he mean by the remark?

In proving that men were in need of salvation, Paul had to show the Jew, especially that he was a sinner. In the second place he had to make him see that he could not be saved by the law. These he did by appealing to their records, declaring that they related to those who were under the law in particular; hence, that the Jew as well as the Gentile was lost and in need of salvation. Therefore it was as a witness to the condition of the people that the law was established.

But I am told that very respectable commentators regard the law here referred to as the moral law, taught in the Old Testament. This, however, does not make it true. And if it did it would not furnish any aid or comfort to Adventism, since we have seen that the Sabbath would not belong to the last; being a positive and not a moral commandment. But it is not possible to accept the common version and regard the law here mentioned as simply those eternal principles which a man must do or not be just before God, for we are to be justified without the deeds of this law. No, it is as a witness that the law is confirmed by the establishment of this Remedial system, by which alone it was possible for men to be saved. The law was given as a whole, and for a definite purpose, of teaching and governing that people till the Christ should come. To have caused it to fail of that purpose would have been to destroy the law, but to cause it to answer that purpose, by bringing in that salvation for which it prepared the people, was to fulfill it. Hence, to fulfill, to establish, or confirm, the law was the work of Christ in giving the gospel to the world, by which the world could be saved. The law and instruction of the pedagogue is established by the higher teacher, when his lessons and rules are declared to have been right. But no one thinks that this leaves the student under the old schoolmaster. If you yet have any doubt of the subject, return and read the third chapter of the Roman letter, beginning at the ninth verse. Then, after quoting freely from some of the prophets and the Psalms, he says, verse 19: "Now we know that what things soever the law saith, it saith to them who are under the law: that every mouth may be stopped, and all the world may become guilty before God."

There is nothing unusual in this use of the word *law*. Many times different parts of the Old Testament are called law. Both prophecy and history are so denominated.

5. *It is said that Paul has plainly declared to the Hebrews that a Sabbath remains to the people of God;* and that as there never was but one Sabbath given to men, to be kept by them, it follows that he intended them to understand that they were yet to observe the seventh day of the week as it was given at Sinai.

According to the new Revision, in Heb. 4:9, we should read: "There remaineth therefore a Sabbath rest for the people of God."

Let us read the whole passage from the first verse: "Let us fear therefore, lest haply, a promise being left of entering into His rest, any one of you should seem to have come short of it. For indeed we have had good tidings preached unto us, even also as they: but the word of hearing did not profit them, because they were not united by faith with them that heard. For we which have believed do enter into that rest; even as he hath said,

    As I sware in my wrath,

    They shall not enter into my rest:

although the works were finished from the foundation of the world. For he hath said somewhere of the seventh day on this wise, And God rested on the seventh day from all his works; and in this place again,

    They shall not enter into my rest.

Seeing therefore it remaineth that some should enter thereinto, and they to whom the good tidings were before preached failed to enter in because of disobedience, he again defineth a certain day, saying in David, after so long a time, To-day, as it hath been before said,

    To-day if ye shall hear his voice,

    Harden not your hearts.

For if Joshua had given them rest, he would not have spoken afterward of another day. There remaineth therefore a Sabbath rest for the people of God. For he that is entered into his rest hath himself also rested from his works, as God did from his. Let us therefore give diligence to enter into that rest, that no man fall after the same example of disobedience."—Verses 1-11.

That this language can have no reference to the weekly Sabbath is evident from the following reasons:

(1) This rest was a *promise* made to them.—v. 1, 6, 8, 9, 10, 11.

(2) It had been promised to *Israel*.—v. 2. The Sabbath had been *commanded* of them, but never *promised*. Commands and promises are very different.

(3) They had the *Sabbath*, but they did not have *this rest*.

(4) Neither did Joshua give them this rest. Yet they had, and kept the Sabbath while he was with them.

(5) As they kept the seventh day, speaking in David of another day, renders it impossible that this rest can refer to the Sabbath which they already had. That day at its best could only be a type of the rest here promised. And like all the types and shadows of the law, disappeared when the New Institution was ushered in.

6. *In the new earth state, they tell us, there will be the Sabbath. To prove this they quote Is.* 66:23.

Let us turn and read the connection that we may understand the subject before the mind of the prophet. See verses 20-23:

"And they shall bring all your brethren for an offering unto the Lord out of all nations, upon horses, and in chariots, and in litters, and upon mules, and upon swift beasts, to my holy mountain Jerusalem, saith the Lord, as the children of Israel bring an offering in a clean vessel into the house of the Lord. And I will also take of them for priests and for Levites, saith the Lord. For as the new heavens and the new earth, which I will make, shall remain before me, saith the Lord, so shall your seed and your name remain. And it shall come to pass, that from one new moon to another, and from one Sabbath to another, shall all flesh come to worship before me, saith the Lord."

It is assumed that this new earth state has reference to the Christian dispensation, and hence that in it the Sabbath shall be as prominent an institution as it was under the law of Moses.

It will be noticed, however, by every one who reads to understand the meaning of the Scripture, that if this text gives any assurance of the continuance of the Sabbath, it as certainly perpetuates the "*new moons.*" The new moon is used in the sense that it is in the law of Moses. Upon the use of this phraseology let the reader turn and read Num. 10:10; 28:2; 1 Chron. 23:31; 2 Chron. 2:4; Is. 1:13; Ez. 45:17; Hos. 2:11.

As we know that the "*new moons*" are not to be observed in the kingdom of Christ, we know that these Sabbaths here spoken of do not refer to that period, or the expression is only a figure to indicate that the habit of worship will be general.

7. *A seventh argument in favor of the Sabbath is made by repeating the word commandment, and always referring it to the Decalogue.* The average Advent lecturer hangs his chart on the wall, and every time he can find the word command or commandment, he points to the chart, as if to impress it upon the minds of the hearers that they are being spoken of. With them, for a man to sin he must absolutely violate law, and that he cannot do where there is no law. Hence, because Adam sinned, he must have violated the ten commandments. They can think of no law but that of the Decalogue. So I suppose as the angels sinned and kept not their first estate, they must have had the ten commandments up in heaven, Sabbath and all, a long time before the world was created, or anything done that was to be memorialized by that institution. This is the extreme of folly to which such a theory will drive even good men.

Turn to Matt. 5:27; 7:26, and get a fair view of the manner in which such terms are employed in the New Testament. Christ first says that "you have heard that it hath been said of old time," "But I say unto you." And after repeating this a good many times, he pronounces a blessing upon those who "hear these sayings of mine and do them."

This is the meaning in Rev. 22:14: "Blessed are they that do his commandments." They were recognized as being under the authority of Christ, the King of kings and Lord of lords. So in the 26th verse of 2nd chapter, "And he that overcometh and keepeth my works unto the end, to him will I give power over the nations." The same thought is found in the third chapter of this book (7-11), in keeping my word, "the word of my patience." In Matt. 10:40, Jesus says: "He that receiveth you receiveth me; and he that receiveth me, receiveth him that sent me." If we would receive the Father, we must receive the Son, and if we would receive the Son we must receive those whom the Son has sent into the world.

This shows plainly, that the only authority in religion recognized on the earth, is that of the Christ.

Matthew 28:18-20: "And Jesus came and spake unto them, saying, all power is given unto me in heaven and earth. Go ye therefore and teach all nations, baptizing them in the name of the Father, and of the Son, and of the Holy Ghost: teaching them to observe all things whatsoever I have commanded you: and lo, I am with you alway, even to the end of the world."

The only things which the apostles had any commission to teach the disciples to keep, were the things he had commanded them to teach. They were not the commandments of Moses nor of the Decalogue, but the things which Christ had commanded.

John 14:21-23: "He that hath my commandments, and keepeth them, he it is that loveth me: and he that loveth me shall be loved of my Father, and I will love him, and will manifest myself to him. . . . . Jesus answered and said unto him, If a man love me he will keep my words, and my Father will love him, and we will come unto him, and will make our abode with him." Verses 15 and 16 of this chapter has the same thought: "If ye love me, keep my commandments, and I will pray the Father, and he shall give you another Comforter, that he may abide with you forever." Read also John 15:10-14; Acts 17:30, 31; 1 John 3:22-24; 1 Cor. 2:1, 2; Rev. 6:9; 12:17; 14:12.

These are a fair sample of the New Testament use of the word commandment. They show that the salvation of the world depends not on keeping the commands of the law, but by hearing what Jesus says and doing what he has commanded.

True the Master has required us to observe many of the things that may be found in the law of Moses; even the golden rule, he says, was taken from the Law and the Prophets. But they are before us as matters of authority not because they were in the law of Moses or in the Decalogue, but because they were commanded by the Lord Jesus Christ. If he had commanded us to keep the Sabbath, then we should have done so, but since he did not, we are perfectly free from any obligation to that institution.

CHAPTER V.

IS THE DECALOGUE YET BINDING?

After it has been made to appear that there is no direct proof of the binding authority of the Sabbath, the friends of that institution undertake to sustain it in this indirect way. Of course, if the Decalogue is binding upon Christians, and we know the Sabbath to have been a part of it, then we must be under law to God to keep it.

1. It is first said that any other position than this frees the religious world from all moral obligation. If we are not under that law, then we may bear false witness, steal, commit adultery, kill, dishonor our parents, covet, etc., etc. That being free from this law, we would be at liberty to commit all the things which it forbade.

This always seemed to me a strange thing, that any one could be found who would have no more regard for logic. The only question is, does the New Testament condemn these things? If it does, then no Christian is at liberty to do them. And every one at all acquainted with that volume knows that each one of these crimes is condemned by the Master and by his apostles with greater clearness and force than they were in the law given at Sinai. Jesus not only taught the other nine commandments, but he gave to them features which they never had before. For the sake of illustration, let us turn to Matt. 5: 27-32, and see how he treats the question of adultery: "Ye have heard that it was said," etc., "but I say unto you, that whosoever looketh on a woman to lust after her, hath committed adultery already with her in his heart." Then he shows them that whatever would lead them into such lust, they must put away from them. Not only so, but he who marries a woman not properly divorced, or divorced for any other cause than her companion's unfaithfulness, commits adultery.

Again, read verses 33-37 of this same chapter, on the subject of profanity. "Ye have heard that it hath been said by them of old time, Thou shalt not forswear thyself. . . . . But I say to you." Then follow directions, showing to them that many were guilty of profanity who never suspected it by reading the law.

Read what he has said on *killing*, in verses 21-26: "Ye have heard that it was said by them of old time, Thou shalt not kill. . . . . But I say to you, that whosoever is angry with his brother without cause shall be in danger of the judgment." And the apostle John tells us that he who hates his brother is a murderer.

If you want to see the Master's way of condemning idolatry or presenting the first commandment, read Matt. 4: 10; John 17: 3; and if you would have a sample of the way in which the apostles condemned this sin, read Acts 14: 8-15; Eph. 4: 6; Rev. 4: 10, 11.

The second command is sustained in Acts 15: 28, 29; Rom. 8: 3, 4; I. John 5: 20, 21; I. Thess. 1: 9.

Profanity, the third thing prohibited in the Decalogue, is condemned in Matt. 5: 33-37, and in James 5: 12.

In Matt. 19: 18, 19, Jesus sustains five commandments, in the following order—6, 7 8, 9, 5. In Rom. 13: 9, Paul presents five commandments in this order—7, 6, 8, 9, 10.

While, therefore, the authors of the New Testament gave but little if any heed to the order in which they occur in the Decalogue, they teach nine out of the ten of these commandments. But while they teach and thus bind these nine upon us, they do not do so because they were in that institution, but because they were right.

No man is able to mention any sin which is not condemned in the New Testament.

2. *It is affirmed that James teaches Christians to be in obedience to the Decalogue, and calls it the Royal Law.*

The language referred to is found in James 2: 8-13. But it is very far from teaching what they affirm it to teach. Let us read it:

"If ye fulfil the royal law according to the Scripture, Thou shalt love thy neighbor as thyself, thou shalt do well: but if ye have respect to persons, ye commit sin, and are convinced of the law as transgressors. For whosoever shall keep the whole law, and yet offend in one point, he is guilty of all. For he that said, Do not commit adultery, said also, Do not kill. Now if thou commit no adultery, yet if thou kill, thou art become a transgressor of the law. So speak ye, and so do, as they that shall be judged by the law of liberty. For he shall have judgment without mercy, that hath showed no mercy; and mercy rejoiceth against judgment."

Now we find no such thing in this passage as that which they affirm. When James speaks of the royal law, or the perfect law of liberty, he mentions only those things which Christ had endorsed and bound upon the disciples. And especially, "Love thy neighbor as thyself," is not in the Decalogue, and yet he gives it as the royal law, which if we fulfill we shall do well. And if we offend in any one feature of it—love to our neighbor —we are guilty. So now, though we are under a system in which mercy rejoices against judgment, and are therefore to be judged by the perfect law of liberty, yet we must so live as God has indicated in giving to us this great law of love.

No one doubts that this royal law is the perfect law of liberty by which we are to be judged. Hence to know certainly what is meant by it, we have only to stop and inquire as to the law under which we shall be judged. A few texts of Scripture may therefore assist in determining this matter.

John 5:22: "The Father has committed all judgment unto the Son."

Acts 17:31: "God has appointed a day in the which he will judge the world in righteousness, by that man whom he hath ordained. . . . Of this he has given assurance unto all men in that he hath raised him up again from the dead."

Romans 2:16: "When God shall judge the secrets of men's hearts by my gospel"—that is, the gospel which he had preached and was even then writing to them.

2 Timothy 4:1: Christ shall "judge the quick and the dead at his appearing and kingdom."

Hebrews 10:30: "The Lord shall judge his people."

1 Peter 1:17: This judgment will be by the Father, and yet as we have learned already it is to be accomplished by the Son.

All through the book of Revelation Christ is represented as the judge.

From Heb. 10:28, 29, we learn that those who live under the light of the New Institution shall be judged by it, and if those who disobeyed the "Old Law, died without mercy under two or three witnesses, there will be still a sorer punishment awarded to those who shall have trampled under foot the Son of God, and counted the blood of the covenant wherewith he was sanctified an unholy thing, and thus done despite to the Spirit of grace."

The teaching of the whole of the New Testament on this subject is that those who lived under the law shall be judged by the law, and that those who lived without law, are to be judged according to the light which they had. But those who live under the New Testament shall be judged by it. Hence we know that the perfect law of liberty is the New Testament.

3. *Such texts as speak of the knowledge of sin coming by the law, are eagerly seized upon as affording some aid and comfort for the doctrine of Adventism.*

The mere fact that an apostle mentions the law, is by them taken as proof that the law was then in existence as a binding force in the minds of these inspired men. When Paul says: "I had not known sin but by the law," he speaks of his early condition as a son of Jewish parents. Hence, like all other persons who were trained and educated under the law, it was from that source that he had his early training concerning right and wrong. But what this may have to do in proving that the law yet remains as a rule by which Christians should live, can only be seen by some one who is bound to find proof of his doctrine and knows of no other place to look for it. We know that the law of Christ condemns every sin which men can commit; that it is much more thorough than the law of Moses ever was, in this respect. Hence we know that no man has to go to the Old Institution to learn what sin is. Certainly Paul—as an apostle—did not have to go to that law to become acquainted with sin. One who was inspired would be under no such obligation. In the days of Paul, the law of Moses was known to those to whom he addressed his epistles, and there were judaizing teachers who were trying to make them believe that they must keep that law. Hence Paul referred to it as an instrument which was known. But he nowhere taught that Christians were under obligations to keep it.

4. *It is sometimes maintained that the long continuance promised to the law, precludes the possibility of its removal.* Moses says

that "secret things belong unto the Lord, but his revealed will belongs unto us and to our children forever, that we may do all the words of this law."

But this *forever* concerns the rite of circumcision and sacrifice as much as the ten commandments. And, therefore, if their application of this and kindred passages be correct, the whole institution is bound upon us. This is true in all those passages they refer to with this supposed proof in it. Nay, more, it would prove that their children would live forever. But if this expression shall be understood to mean descendants, then how do they find that the law is the common property of all the nations?

The truth is, that the same, or even stronger terms are used concerning circumcision alone. It was to be a mark between God and that people forever. Does this mean that circumcision is bound upon all people for all time? To ask the question, is to receive from every one a negative answer.

5. *It is unreasonable, they tell us, that God should have given a law to man, and then afterwards become ashamed of that law and torn it down.*

And yet if I ask one of these men to be circumcised, he refuses. But why refuse? Was not God the author of circumcision? I ask him to offer two rams and a bullock in order that he may be consecrated to the priesthood, but he says, no indeed. But why so? Did not God give that law?

But he says that all the judiciary and ritual were done away. Where, then, is that argument? It was founded on the fact that God had given that law and, therefore, it must remain forever. But we have a large number of laws from God which he says has been done away. Since then, he knows that God may have given law to last but for a given time and to accomplish a given purpose, the wonderful argument is gone.

6. *The Decalogue was written on tables of stone, by the finger of God.*

But what has that to do with its perpetuity? Was not any other law uttered by Jehovah, either directly, or indirectly, of equal authority? Are the ten commandments any more the law of God after they were written on tables of stone than when uttered by God from the summit of Mt. Sinai? What is
3

there in the fact that the Decalogue was written on tables of stone by the finger of God that makes it more his law than anything else which he commanded that people?

They say that there were two laws, one from Moses and the other from God. Every time they can find the word Moses to any part of the ancient revelation, then that is of Moses, but the other refers to the ten commandments. Moses is the author of one of these, while the other is God's law. They claim that the law of Moses was done away, but the law of God remains forever.

This makes Moses a better law-giver than God himself. The lawyer that tempted the Master, wished to know which was the great commandment of the law. Jesus told him that it was to love the Lord with all his heart and soul and mind, and to love his neighbor as himself. Neither of these is to be found in the Decalogue and yet they were chief. That is not all, a man might observe every one of the ten, and not keep either one of these. Thus, in their mad haste, they will do away with the very principles which are eternal, simply to make room for a hobby about keeping a certain day!

Upon the basis which they urge, for two laws, it would be perfectly easy to find that there are two Gods. They find that there are different things said about the law, therefore there must be two laws. Just like it would be to find that because God is spoken of as our Father, and also as a fierce lion, as a man of war, therefore there must be two Gods. Christ says, I came not to judge the world. And then again he says, that God hath committed all judgment to the Son. Their logic will compel us to suppose from these statements that there are two Christs. The whole blunder comes from having a hobby which finds no other means of support than by a scrap system, that snatches texts out of their connection simply to sustain a theory. In this way any doctrine may be sustained. Any lawyer would be disbarred from the practice of law if he persisted in such a use of our statute.

I want here to make a quotation from Alexander Campbell. I do this for two reasons, (1) Mr. Campbell expresses our views very clearly, and (2) Advent preachers are in the habit of saying that Mr. Campbell knew that the seventh day was the day to keep; and toward the close of his life, indicated that it should be done. While there could be nothing more false than this, still there are many persons who are imposed upon by their statements.

I quote from Lectures on the Pentateuch, p. 271, 272:

"There remains another objection to this division of the law. It sets itself in opposition to the skill of an apostle, and ultimately deters us from speaking of the ten precepts as he did. Paul, according to the wisdom given to him, denominated the ten precepts, the ministration of condemnation and of death. 2 Cor. 3:7, 14. This we call the moral law. Whether he or we are to be esteemed the most able ministers of Christ, it remains for you, my friends, to say. Paul, having called the ten precepts the ministration of death, next affirmed that it was to be 'done away,' and that it 'was done away.' Now, the calling the ten precepts 'the moral law,' is not only a violation of the use of the word; is not only inconsistent in itself, and contradictory to truth; but greatly obscures the doctrine taught by the apostle in the third chapter of 2 Corinthians, and in similar passages, so as to render it almost, if not altogether, unintelligible to us."

I quote again from page 286: "'Sin,' says the apostle, 'shall not have dominion over you; for ye are not under the law, but under grace.' In the sixth and seventh chapters to the Romans, the apostle taught them that they were not under the law but under grace; that they were freed from it—'dead to it'—'delivered from it.' In the eighth chapter, first verse, he draws the above conclusion. What a pity that modern teachers should have added to, and clogged the words of inspiration by such unauthorized sentences as the following: 'Ye are not under the law as a covenant of works, but as a rule of life.' Whoever read one word of 'the covenant of works' in the Bible, or of the Jewish law being a rule of life to the disciples of Christ? Of these you hear no more from the Bible than of the 'Solemn League' or of 'St. Giles' day.'"

Again, from page 288: "But query: Is the Law of Moses a rule of life to Christians? An advocate of the popular doctrine replies, 'Not all of it.' Query again: What part of it? 'The ten commandments.' Are these a rule of life to Christians?

'Yes.' Should not, then, Christians sanctify the seventh day? 'No.' Why so? 'Because Christ has not enjoined it.' Oh! then, the law, or ten commandments, is not a rule of life to Christians any further than it is enjoined by Christ; so that in reading the precepts in Moses' words, or hearing him utter them, does not oblige us to observe them—it is only what Christ says we must observe. So that an advocate for the popular doctrine, when closely pressed, can not maintain his ground."

There is no greater mistake than to suppose that a part of the law was left binding, as a law, while the rest of it was taken away. Their division of it, is purely fanciful. The Bible knows nothing about it. Jesus treated the ten commandments just as he did the rest of the law; it had served its purpose as a constitution of a national religion. The government which was built upon it was both political and religious. And as a whole system, the law had served its purpose in preparing the people for the higher lessons of the Great Teacher.

7. *But they sometimes ask, why would God take away the ten commandments in order to get rid of one? Why not blot out the one and leave the other nine standing?*

Whatever may be the impression such a question may make on the mind of a Bible reader, we must treat it gravely, for they all ask it, supposing evidently that it has some element of strength. Again we might ask if God removed all the law but the ten commandments? To which they are bound to answer yes. We ask again if many of the things now in the Christian Institution, were not in the law of Moses? Again they say yes. Then why were these things taken away? Why were they not left standing, seeing they must be in the New Covenant as well as in the Old? From this it will appear that they are just as much in need of showing why God has first removed and then re-enacted as we are. Here is the simple truth in the premises: God has taught men as they have been capable of receiving instruction. He has also made requirements of them as they had more light and more responsibility. Many things in the Patriarchal system was put into Judaism. That fact, however, did not leave the Jew under the Patriarchal religion, nor under any part of it as having appeared there. He gave them a new law. Yet not new in all its forms and principles; and yet they were bound only to observe these things because they were in the law of Moses, and not because they had been given to the Patriarchs.

So it was in the establishment of the covenant of Christ, God gave a law as perfectly new, as if there had never been a law given since the foundation of the world. But in this law of faith, this perfect law of liberty, it pleased him to give us many things which had been in the Patriarchal and Jewish systems, and they are now binding upon us, not because they were there, but because they are here; not because they were of the fathers or of Moses, but because they are of Christ.

Before our states came into the union as states, they had forms of territorial government. When they were admitted as states, they came in with a constitution on which could be based a code for the government of the people. In that code there have been many things which had previously been in the territorial code. And yet the law is as wholly independent of the territorial law as if no such law had ever existed. So it was with the law of Moses, it served its purpose, and passed away, to make room for a universal religion. As Paul says: "He took away the first that he might establish the second."—Heb. 10:9.

8. *An eighth argument by the friends of the Sabbath is that the Decalogue was declared by the Lord to be perfect, and that God said of the rest of the law that it was not good.*

In the first place, God never said that the Decalogue was perfect. It is said of the Law of the Lord, that it was perfect, converting the soul (Ps. 19:7). But it would be the law of love, not found in the Decalogue, that would convert the soul. As to the perfection of that law, Jesus shows very clearly that it was not. He added to it in the very things which he retained. It was perfect, however, for the work which it was to perform. It was only given as a pedagogue to lead that people during the days of their minority.

We should not be surprised to hear an infidel quote Ez. 20:25, to prove that God had purposely injured his people whom he had pledged himself to protect and save. But when any class of professed believers make the same use of it, we are ready to ask: "Where is thy faith?" But I will quote the text:

" I lifted up mine hand unto them also in the wilderness, that

I would scatter them among the heathen, and disperse them through the countries; because they had not executed my judgments, but had despised my statutes, and had polluted my sabbaths, and their eyes were after their fathers' idols. Wherefore I gave them also statutes that were not good, and judgments whereby they should not live; and I polluted them in their own gifts, in that they caused to pass through the fire all that openeth the womb, that I might make them desolate to the end that they might know that I am the Lord."—Ez. 20 : 23-26.

Of course this law can have nothing to do with the law given at Mt. Sinai, for it was after that they had violated the very law that was there given. Indeed it was after that they had introduced those gross forms of idolatry, such as burning their children, in the service of their heathen deities. It was many years after they had come into the promised land that they did such things as are here named. Hence it follows that God simply permitted them to receive the reward of their own doings that they might learn the results. And through the nations to which he permitted them to be sold in bondage, they received those laws which were not good.

In this again is seen the usual weakness of the system which compels its defenders into the work of scrapping the Scriptures and using the word of God for its sound and not for its sense.

CHAPTER VI.

THE LAW OF WHICH THE SABBATH WAS A PART WAS DONE AWAY IN CHRIST.

I. My first witness is Jeremiah 31 : 31-34 : "Behold the days come, saith the Lord, that I will make a new covenant with the house of Israel and with the house of Judah : not according to the covenant that I made with their fathers, in the day that I took them by the hand to bring them out of the land of Egypt; which my covenant they break, although I was an husband unto them saith the Lord : but this shall be the covenant that I will make with the house of Israel after those days, saith the Lord :

I will put my law in their inward parts, and write it in their hearts; and will be their God, and they shall be my people. And they shall teach no more every man his neighbor, and every man his brother, saying, Know the Lord: for they shall all know me, from the least of them unto the greatest of them, saith the Lord: for I will forgive their iniquity, and I will remember their sin no more."

Now when we read Heb. 8:6-13, we have Paul quoting this and applying it to the covenant of Christ. He shows by the quotation that the covenant made with the fathers was old when Jeremiah wrote this language; not only that it was old, but that it was ready to vanish away. Hence, according to the promise of God, it had vanished away, and a new covenant had come to take its place. Between the covenant made by Christ and that made with the fathers at Mount Sinai, there are several distinctions.

(1) That was old and this is new. (2) This is not according to that. (3) That law was written on tables of stone and on papyri, but this is put into the hearts of the people. (4) In *that* covenant there were many who did not know the Lord, but in *this* they all know him, from the least to the greatest. (5) *That* was national but this is to be universal, and to be constituted of those who have first heard and learned of the Lord. (6) In *this* covenant sins once forgiven are remembered no more; but in *that*, there was a remembrance of sins once every year.

But they tell us that this covenant made with the fathers was the ritual and judicial law, and not the law of the ten commandments. This, however, is only assumed. God never divided the law, nor made any such distinctions in it as they do.

Again they say that the covenant here spoken of was "*made*," and that the covenant of the ten commandments was a covenant that was "*commanded*." This is a distinction without a difference. All covenants that have been given by the Lord, have been commanded. When God gave the seed of Abraham the covenant of circumcision, he gave it in the form of the imperative. So it was with all the features of all the covenants which he has ever made with his creatures. On one side of the contract, God has made certain promises, and on the other, he has required certain duties. Then it has been left to men to say if they would accept of the conditions or not. Hence, all their talk about covenants "*made*" and covenants "*commanded*" darkens counsel by multiplying words.

Exodus 34:10, 11: "And he said, Behold, I *make* a covenant: before all thy people I will do marvels, such as have not been done in all the earth, nor in any nation: and all the people among which thou art shall see the work of the Lord: for it is a terrible thing that I will do with thee. Observe thou that which I *command* thee this day."

This is the usual form: God *makes* his promises to them, on the one hand, and *commands* their obedience to his will on the other.

Read the 27th and 28th verses of this chapter and we will find the very word "*made*" employed in reference to the ten commandments: "And the Lord said unto Moses, Write these words: for after the tenor of these words I have *made* a covenant with thee and with Israel. And he was there with the Lord forty days and forty nights; he did neither eat bread nor drink water. And he wrote upon the tables the words of the covenant, the ten commandments."

Here the ten commandments are said especially to be the covenant which God "*made*" with Moses and with Israel. We have already seen in Deut. 4:8; 5:3-15, that this very covenant of ten commandments was included in the contract which God made with his people. "*Made*" is the word which God himself selected by which to indicate the giving of the ten commandments.

Still further, it is evident that the Decalogue is not supposed to be absent in this reference of Jeremiah, for he puts in contrast or antithesis, the writing of the new covenant in the hearts of the people, and the writing of the old covenant in some other way. This is so much like the reference to the same subject in Paul's second letter to the church at Corinth, in which the antithetical writing was said to have been done on tables of stone, that it is most natural to give it that meaning here. In every way, therefore, our first witness stands secure. And he leaves us without doubt concerning the fact that the law, as an entirety, was to be taken away in Christ, and that it *was* taken away when he was crucified.

II. Paul, in his letter to the Hebrews, furnishes the testimony which we next introduce:

Hebrews 7:11, 12: "If therefore perfection were by the Levitical priesthood, (for under it the people received the law,) what further need was there that another priest should arise after the order of Melchizedek, and not be called after the order of Aaron? For the priesthood being changed, there is made of necessity a change also of the law."

Of course the defenders of the Sabbath feel that they have done enough when they have denied that the law here referred to includes the ten commandments. But this denial is utterly without reason. There are no evidences to be found in the whole epistle that the apostle thought of such a separation of the law as that which they make in order to sustain their theory. He shows that the whole system has been changed, and that a change in one respect made the change in every other, an absolute necessity.

Exodus 24:4-8: "And Moses wrote all the words of the Lord, and rose up early in the morning, and builded an altar under the hill, and twelve pillars, according to the twelve tribes of Israel. And he sent young men of the children of Israel, which offered burnt offerings, and sacrificed peace offerings of oxen unto the Lord. And Moses took half of the blood, and put it in basins; and half of the blood he sprinkled on the altar. And he took the book of the covenant, and read in the audience of the people: and they said, All that the Lord hath said will we do and be obedient. And Moses took the blood, and sprinkled it on the people, and said, Behold the blood of the covenant, which the Lord hath made with you concerning all these words."

In this law there was the ten commandments and an amplification of them. To see just what this roll contained, we should turn and read from the beginning of the 20th chapter. This discourse contained the teaching of God to that people as a fundamental law, or a constitution for them in their national organization, and was what Moses wrote in a book and enjoined upon them.

Now we turn to Heb. 9:15-19: "And for this cause he is the Mediator of the New Testament, that by means of death, for the redemption of the transgressions that were under the First Testament (covenant), they which are called might receive the promise of eternal inheritance. For where a testament is, there must also of necessity be the death of the testator (testament sacrifice). For a testament is of force after men are dead: otherwise it hath no strength at all while the testator liveth. Whereupon neither the First Testament was dedicated without blood. For when Moses had spoken every precept to all the people according to the law, he took the blood of calves and of goats, with water, and scarlet wool, and hyssop, and sprinkled both the book and all the people, saying, This is the blood of the testament which God hath enjoined unto you."

Here Paul can have reference only to that law spoken of in Ex. 24. Hence he has now very clearly before him the First and the Second Testaments: The one given by Moses, and the New Covenant—of the Messiah. This First was the ten commandments and a proper elaboration, showing their bearing upon all the details of life. But now what is said to have been done with this old covenant, this First Testament? Read right along till you reach the 9th verse of the 10th chapter, where he shows that Christ became the sum of all divine authority, for whose covenant the first was removed. This is what is said:

"Then said he: Lo, I come to do thy will, O God. He taketh away the first, that he may establish the second."

The only first and second of which the apostle has spoken in this whole connection, are the two testaments, that given through Moses, containing the Decalogue, and that given by the Christ. Hence, with these facts clearly before us, when Paul says, "He taketh away the first, that he may establish the second," he means, for there is nothing else that he can mean, that he took away that old institution, Decalogue and all, that he might establish the New Covenant, the covenant of Christ.

III. *My third witness is Paul in his letter to the Ephesians.* Chapter 2:14, 15: "For he is our peace, who hath made both one, and hath broken down the middle wall of partition between us; having abolished in his flesh the enmity, even the law of commandments contained in ordinances; for to make in himself of twain one new man, so making peace."

Here, as in his letter to the Hebrews, Paul shows that all that held that old national organization together and made it distinctive, was removed, that in Christ, both Jews and Gentiles might be united in one body, in which peace should obtain.

IV. *A fourth witness is the testimony of Paul to the brethren in Galatia.*

In chapter two and verse 19, he says: "For I through the law am dead to the law, that I might live unto God."

Galatians 3:16-25: "Now to Abraham and to his seed were the promises made. He saith not, And to seeds, as of many; but as of one, And to thy seed, which is Christ. And this I say, that the covenant, that was confirmed before of God in Christ, the law, which was four hundred and thirty years after, cannot disannul, that it should make the promise of none effect. For if the inheritance be of the law, it is no more of promise: but God gave it to Abraham by promise. Wherefore then serveth the law? It was added because of transgressions, till the seed should come to whom the promise was made; and it was ordained by angels in the hand of a mediator. Now a mediator is not a mediator of one, but God is one. Is the law then against the promises of God? God forbid: for if there had been a law given which could have given life, verily righteousness should have been by the law. But the Scripture hath concluded all under sin, that the promise by faith of Jesus Christ might be given to them that believe. But before faith came, we were kept under the law, shut up unto the faith which should afterwards be revealed. Wherefore the law was our schoolmaster to bring us unto Christ, that we might be justified by faith. But since that faith is come, we are no longer under a schoolmaster."

Now if it is possible for human speech to contain the thought, this language clearly announces the fact, that the law had served its purpose and had stepped aside.

In chapter five and 4th verse, he says: "Christ is become of no effect unto you, whosoever of you are justified by the law; ye are fallen from grace."

Adventists satisfy themselves by saying that the ceremonial law is here meant. No doubt that it is included, but it is not all that is referred to in the language. The righteousness of the law speaketh on this wise: They that do these things shall live by them. It was not therefore alone in the atonement of the law that they were told not to trust, but in the deeds of the law.

Hence, the law as a whole, is said to have served as a schoolmaster, and, having fulfilled the appointment, he was taken out of the way to make room for the law of Christ.

But as the Galatians were peculiarly troubled with Judaizing teachers, Paul gave a great deal of space in this letter to this subject, that they might know they were not under the law that was given their fathers at Mount Sinai, but that they were under law to Christ. But I will conclude this testimony by one more quotation from chapter four and verses 21-31:

"Tell me, ye that desire to be under the law, do ye not hear the law? For it is written, that Abraham had two sons, the one by a bondmaid, the other by a free woman. But he who was of the bondwoman was born after the flesh; but he of the free woman was by promise. Which things are an allegory: for these are the two covenants; the one from the Mount Sinai, which gendereth to bondage, which is Agar. For this Agar is Mount Sinai in Arabia, and answereth to Jerusalem which now is, and is in bondage with her children. But Jerusalem which is above is free, which is the mother of us all. For it is written, Rejoice, thou barren that bearest not; break forth and cry, thou that travailest not; for the desolate hath many more children than she which hath a husband. Now we, brethren, as Isaac was, are the children of promise. But as then he that was born after the flesh, persecuted him that was born after the Spirit, even so it is now. Nevertheless what saith the Scripture? Cast out the bondwoman and her son: for the son of the bondwoman shall not be heir with the son of the free woman. So then, brethren, we are not children of the bondwoman, but of the free."

In this, as in the most the author has said in this epistle and in other places, he makes no difference in the law, but puts all that was in the Sinaitic covenant into one system and represents it by Hagar, and then puts the whole system of redemption in Christ in the other, and represents it by Sarah. And then he says that the bondwoman was to be cast out for she and her son should not be heir with the free woman and her son. Hence, those disciples who were disposed to mix Judaism and Christianity were wrong; these two covenants could not live together.

V. *Paul's indifference to the law, is our fifth witness.*

1 Cor. 9:20, 21: "And unto the Jews I became as a Jew, that I might gain the Jews; to them that are under the law, as under the law, that I might gain them that are under the law; to them that are without the law, as without the law, (being not without law to God, but under the law to Christ), that I might gain them that are without law."

From this it is certain that if Paul was not a hypocrite, he was perfectly indifferent as to keeping the law of the Old Testament. He regarded doing these things as innocent enough, that he could conform to the regulations and prejudices of any community, either to keep these things or let them alone. As he did in the case of Timothy, in circumcising him because of the Jews in those quarters, so he regarded the whole question.

The only law he recognized was the law of Christ. Through his law alone he was under law to God. No Adventist could speak thus of himself. Nor would any one of them ever cite Paul as having made any such a statement as that. It shows that Paul could not have been a Sabbatarian. If some keeper of the Sabbath had been serving as Paul's emanuensis he would have said, "Not so, brother Paul: you should say that you are without law, except that you are under the Decalogue, as well as the commandments of Jesus."

VI. *Our sixth and last argument on the removal of the law, is founded on the opinion of the apostles and elders and the whole church at Jerusalem, in the council reported in Acts, 15th chapter.*

There were Judaizing teachers who taught the disciples that Gentiles could not be saved unless they would be circumcised and keep the law of Moses. They went even as far as to Antioch teaching this doctrine. Paul and others withstood them, and finally it was carried up to Jerusalem to the apostles and elders. And, after a full discussion, and the induction of the facts of revelation on the subject, they reached the unanimous opinion reported in Acts 15:22-31:

"Then pleased it the apostles and elders, with the whole church, to send chosen men of their own company to Antioch, with Paul and Barnabas; namely, Judas surnamed Barsabas, and Silas, chief men among the brethren: And wrote letters by them after this manner, The apostles and elders, and brethren, send greeting unto the brethren which are of the Gentiles in Antioch, and Syria, and Cilicia: Forasmuch as we have heard, that certain which went out from us have troubled you with words, subverting your souls, saying, Ye must be circumcised, and keep the law: to whom we gave no such commandment: It seemed good unto us, being assembled with one accord, to send chosen men unto you, with our beloved Barnabas and Paul; Men that have hazarded their lives for the name of our Lord Jesus Christ. We have sent therefore Judas and Silas, who shall also tell you the same things by mouth. For it seemed good to the Holy Ghost, and to us, to lay upon you no greater burden than these necessary things; that ye abstain from meats offered to idols, and from blood, and from things strangled, and from fornication: from which if ye keep yourselves, ye shall do well. Fare ye well. So when they were dismissed, they came to Antioch: and when they had gathered the multitude together, they delivered the epistle: Which when they had read, they rejoiced for the consolation."

A supreme court decision on any disputed point of law could not be clearer and more satisfactory than this. They recognized only the law of Christ upon them. Even the burdens that seem to have any features of the law in them relate to what Adventists call the ceremonial law. And it is as evident as it can be that there is not a Sabbatarian in the whole land who would have agreed with that council if he had been present. He would have said: "Brethren, this is all wrong; while we are freed from the ceremonial law by the body of Christ, we remain under the ten commandments, and any decision which will not recognize that fact is heresy; not only so, but it will ruin the world, for unless men keep the Sabbath they cannot be saved."

CHAPTER VII.

THE CONCLUSION OF PART FIRST: THE LAW CONTAINING THE SABBATH HAVING PASSED AWAY, THE SABBATH ITSELF HAS NO MORE CLAIM UPON CHRISTIANS THAN ANY OTHER FEATURE OF THE LAW GIVEN TO ISRAEL AT MT. SINAI.

It is evident to every one, that if the law was done which contained the Sabbath, the Sabbath went with it, and, unless it was re-enacted by the Savior, is no more a law by which Christians should be governed than the law of circumcision, which was given alone to the seed of Abraham, and to those bought with their money. Hence it seems proper to continue the evidence upon the question in hand, not because the Scriptures already quoted are insufficient, but that we may add to them a few other statements, exhibiting the fact that in at least half of the epistolary communications, this doctrine of modern Sabbatarianism was directly opposed by inspiration.

VII. *As a seventh testimony on this subject I will quote Romans* 7:1-7.

"Know ye not, brethren, (for I speak to them who know the law,) how that the law hath dominion over a man as long as he liveth? For the woman which hath a husband is bound by the law to her husband so long as he liveth; but if her husband be dead, she is loosed from the law of her husband. So then if, while her husband liveth, she be married to another man, she shall be called an adulteress: but if her husband be dead, she is free from that law; so that she is no adulteress, though she be married to another man. Wherefore, my brethren, ye also are become dead to the law by the body of Christ; that ye should be married to another, even to him who is raised from the dead, that we should bring forth fruit unto God. For when we were in the flesh, the motions of sins, which were by the law, did work in our members to bring forth fruit unto death. But now we are delivered from the law, that, being dead wherein we were held; that we should serve in newness of spirit, and not in the oldness of the letter. What shall we say then? Is the law sin? God forbid. Nay, I had not known sin, but by the law: for I had not known lust, except the law had said, Thou shalt not covet."

Here the teaching is plain: (1) These brethren had once been under the law of Moses—not a part of it, but the whole of it. (2) While that law was in existence they were so related to it that service to any other system would have been regarded as unfaithfulness in a wife to her husband. (3) But as a woman is free from the law of her husband by his death, so they had been made free from the requirements of the law by the body of Christ. (4) Being made free from the law in which they had been held, it was right that they should be married to Christ, and that in this new relation, they should bring forth fruit to God. (5) It is also clear that the law referred to, contained the Decalogue, for the word covet quoted by Paul, is only to be found in that part of the law. Hence, if it is possible for a man to teach anything by the use of words, then has Paul taught in this passage that we are not under the law of Moses in any respect.

VIII. *The eighth witness on this subject will be found by reading* 2 *Cor.* 3 : 5-14.

"But our sufficiency is of God; who also hath made us able ministers of the New Testament; not of the letter, but of the Spirit; for the letter killeth, but the Spirit giveth life. But if the ministration of death, written and engraven in stones, was glorious, so that the children of Israel could not steadfastly behold the face of Moses for the glory of his countenance; which *glory* was to be done away; how shall not the ministration of the Spirit be rather glorious? Seeing then that we have such hope, we use great plainness of speech: And not as Moses, which put a vail over his face, that the children of Israel could not steadfastly look to the end of that which is abolished. But their minds were blinded: for until this day remaineth the same vail untaken away in the reading of the Old Testament; which is done away in Christ."

It will be noticed that I do not use the word *vail* in the last verse. But as it is wholly unwarranted, there being nothing in the original from which it comes, I dismiss it. Our translators have put it in italic letters denoting that it was supplied; but they should not have put it there at all.

In this passage it is said distinctly three several times that the Old Covenant "was done away" (11), "abolished" (13), and "done away in Christ" (14). Now whatever that law was that is here put in antithesis with the gospel of Christ, it had been done away when Paul wrote this epistle. Further, it is impossible that Paul should have had any other writing before his mind in indicating this Scripture than the Decalogue. It was the ministration of death, written and engraven in stones; the Old Testament, and was done away in Christ.

A part of this Old Institution was the Sabbath day, and went with the law of which it was a part, the law having been removed it could not have been left standing. I have never heard anything like an answer to this argument from the friends of the Sabbath. I do not think there is any to be made. Indeed if I were directed to write a statement that the law containing the Sabbath was removed, I could not make it stronger than Paul has in the language just quoted.

IX. *A last witness is taken from Paul's letter to the brethren at Colosse; chapter* 2:13-17.

"And you, being dead in your sins and the uncircumcision of of your flesh, hath he quickened together with him, having forgiven you all trespasses; blotting out the handwriting of ordinances that was against us, which was contrary to us, and took it out of the way, nailing it to the cross; and having spoiled principalities and powers, he made a show of them openly. triumphing over them in it. Let no man therefore judge you in meat, or in drink, or in respect of a holy day, or of the new moon, or of the Sabbath: Which are a shadow of things to come; but the body is of Christ."

Here it will be seen that I have chosen to leave off the italicised word *days*. It is known to every reader that words of the Common Version found in italic letters are without any authority in the Scriptures, and that they have only been put into the body of the work because the compilers thought that the passage would be better understood by their use. But, as in the added *vail* in the Corinthian letter, they are positively in the way of the truth, and therefore better left out.

It is said that the ordinances of this passage belong to the ceremonial law and not to the Decalogue, and hence Paul was not speaking of the removal of the ten commandments.

It will be answer enough to this, to say that the word *dogma*, here translated ordinance, occurs five times in the New Testament, and in three of them it is rendered decree.—Luke 2 : 1 ; Acts 16 : 4 ; 17 : 7. The word does not indicate ceremonies any more than any other edict of a sovereign.

Another attempt to explain away the meaning of the passage is that the word Sabbath means, not the weekly rest-day, but feast days or stated festivals, which belonged to the ceremonial law.

The word, however, rendered holy day (*heortes*), has just that meaning in it and covers all the ground they wish to have the Sabbath occupy in the text. It is rendered literally correct in the Emphatic Diaglott: "Let no one, therefore, rule you in food, or in drink, or in respect of a festival, or of a new moon, or of Sabbaths."

It is therefore as plain as anything can be, that the word Sabbath does not refer to any of the Jewish feast days for they had already been spoken of. And there was nothing else that the writer could have referred to but the Sabbath of the Decalogue.

A kind of last resort is to claim that the word *sabbatoon* is plural, and hence it must be rendered Sabbaths or Sabbath days, and therefore it cannot relate to the weekly Sabbath.

We have already seen that there were no other days that it could have meant, as they were presented in the other words of the text, and there is no reason to suppose that the Sabbatical year or the jubilee be intended. Hence there was nothing else to which reference could have been made.

As for the word Sabbath being the plural, it signifies nothing, since the day occurred over and over again, and might, therefore, be spoken of in the plural number with great propriety.

Still further, it is known to every one who reads the Greek of the New Testament, that the third declension plural—as in the case in hand—is used interchangeably with the second declension singular. And that it is therefore many times rightly rendered by a noun in the singular number. I will refer to a few occurrences of the word in question, that the reader may see just how it is constantly used:

(1) Matt. 12:1: "Jesus went on the *Sabbath* day through the corn."

(2) Verse 11: "And if it fall into a pit on the *Sabbath* day."

(3) "In the end of the *Sabbath*, as it began to dawn toward the first (day) of the week." Here the word week is from *sabbatoon*, neutral, plural, third declension, the same as the word Sabbath.

(4) Mark 1:21: "On the *Sabbath* day he entered into the synagogue and taught."

(5) Mark 11:23: "He went through the corn fields on the *Sabbath* day."

(6) Verse 24: "Why do they on the *Sabbath* day that which is not lawful?"

(7) Mark 3:4: Is it lawful to do good on the *Sabbath* day, or to do evil?"

(8) Mark 16:2: "And very early in the morning of the first (day) of the *week*."

(9) Luke 4:16: "He went into the synagogue on the *Sabbath* day and stood up for to read."

(10) Luke 13:10: "And he was teaching in one of the synagogues on the *Sabbath*."

(11) Luke 24:1: "Now upon the first (day) of the *week*."

(12) John 20:1: "The first (day) of the *week*."

(13) Verse 19: "Then the same day at evening, being the first (day) of the *week*."

(14) Acts 20:7: "And upon the first (day) of the *week*."

(15) 1 Cor. 16:2: "Upon the first (day) of the *week*."

From the foregoing induction, it is as certain as it can be, that there is no sufficient reason for using the word *days* in Col. 11:16, or for demanding that it shall have a plural rendering. Many of the parallel passages of those we cited are second declension singular, and those of the third declension plural, in every case refer to the weekly Sabbath, except those cases in which it is preceded by the adjective *first*, where it is always rendered *week;* the word day being employed to fill the ellipsis. From all that is now before us in respect to this passage we are compelled to say:

1. Paul did not use the word *Sabbath* in the sense of feast

days, for he had just spoken of them in the most appropriate terms possible, and would not repeat it in the same sentence.

2. He speaks of the *weekly Sabbath*, there being nothing else to which he could have spoken.

3. He classes it with other features of the law which had been removed by the cross of Christ.

4. Christians being free from the law with all its demands, are not to be held accountable for the keeping of any of it. As we shall not be judged by a law under which we do not live, we are not to yield to the whims of those who would bring us again into bondage in such matters.

Here I feel disposed to dismiss the case so far as the keeping of the Sabbath is concerned. When Paul says, let no man judge you in respect of the Sabbath, I stand upon that liberty, and do not propose that any man shall entangle me in that service which was taken out of the way and nailed to the cross.

There have been many strange doctrines preached in the name of Christianity, but how any man with ordinary judgment, and any faith at all in the inspiration of the apostles, can claim that we must keep the seventh day of the week, by virtue of the law that was given at Mt. Sinai, when nearly half of the argumentative portion of the epistles was leveled directly against that very falsehood, is exceedingly strange.

In the minds of those who feel that we must have a "*thou shalt*" for all acts of devotion, will feel that we have removed one of the great props by which the world shall be made to respect the service of God. Their fear is wholly unnecessary. We are not going to be injured in any way in following the Scriptures. And we know that if they teach anything, they teach that we are free from the law; that we are not under the law; that the law was done away in Christ; that it only served as a schoolmaster to bring us to Christ that we might be justified by faith, but that as faith has come, we are no longer under the old schoolmaster. Nay, more, the conclusion is drawn for us; these things being so, this law having been taken away, we are not to be judged by anything which it contained: new moons, feast days, or the Sabbath.

Still it will be asked if the Sabbath to the Jew was not a foundation for the Lord's day to be observed by the Christian?

While it may be true that it is best for men to take one day out of every seven for rest and devotion, we will see in the second proposition that the two days are very unlike in many particulars. They were for different purposes and kept for different reasons. The one called to mind the creation of the world and the delivery of Israel from Egypt, while the other recalls the redemption that is in Christ Jesus and his promise to come a second time without a sin offering to salvation.

PART SECOND.

THE LORD'S DAY.

CHAPTER I.

THE SOURCE OF KNOWLEDGE.

We have now seen that the New Testament gives no authority for the observance of the seventh day of the week as a day of rest, any more than it warrants us in keeping any other day. Hence, to observe it as a day of rest, will be simply as keeping any other form of tradition or of the commandments of men, and in the second chapter of Colossians it is so ranked by the Apostle Paul. But the question now before us is, shall we observe any day? If so, which one of the seven? and how shall we be able to determine?

We have two ways of knowing the will of the Lord: first, God has stated directly many things he would have us do; and second, he has presented before us in the lives of his inspired servants, examples for us to copy

In all ages of the church the best minds have ever agreed that to live, as did the early churches, under the eye and sanction of the apostles, will be pleasing and acceptable to God. From which of these sources must we expect intelligence concerning the day we are to keep? The Sabbatarian, regarding himself as under the law of Moses, has trained himself only to expect intelligence in a direct command, and to regard nothing as sacred which does not come in that way.

God has taught the world as we teach our children, always regarding the age and condition of those to be instructed. When we instruct our children, we proceed as God did in the patriarchal times, and in the law of Moses; we state duties without assigning the reasons for them, simply because those we are instructing are incompetent to lay hold of the principles that are to guide them in their conduct. But these were primary institutions, serving as man's teachers, preparing for Christ, the great teacher, under whose instructions we may graduate for the heavens. The manner of teaching, therefore, that was proper during the days of Moses, cannot be expected to be continued in the new Institution. When we have reached our majority in Christ, in the new covenant, we are treated as though we were competent to learn truth, not only by direct statement, but by example become acquainted not only with facts, but with principles that shall guide us in the service of the Lord. For these higher lessons, God was preparing the world during the ages. His provisions and revelations were upon the basis of man's necessities. God revealed his will, his love, and his power in those systems of relief and blessing which were temporal in themselves, but which, in their typology, looked to him who is the perfect Law-giver.

Man's first want was that of knowledge, and to supply that want, God sent a prophet, or a line of prophets, all of whom were anointed or christed. These were the agents through whom the divine will was made known, and this want of man supplied. Man's second want was pardon. He knew himself to be guilty and, therefore, suffered from a consciousness of sins and fearful looking for of judgment and fiery indignation. To relieve man of this weakness, provision was made for pardon in an atoning sacrifice offered by a priest, year by year, but-this priest, or these priests, must be anointed or christed before they could serve.

Man's third want was a guide, a governor, a protector. When the people of Israel asked God to give them a king, the demand was a purely human one, and was made from that felt necessity of some one to control them and protect them from their enemies. But before a king could serve them, he must be anointed or christed. So, while God supplied their then present wants, he was furnishing instructions concerning the coming One who should, in himself, answer all human necessities, being the prophet, the priest and king, teaching, governing and saving the world.

We learn Christ's will not only by what he said, but by what he did and the things which he approved. Had he never said anything relative to marriage, his presence at the wedding in Cana of Galilee, and remaining during the feast, would show his approval of that relation. After teaching his apostles for more than three years, there were many things that had not been told them; many things which they could not understand; and when he went away, he gave them the promise of another Comforter, another Helper, who should guide them into all truth; who should receive of him and deliver to them, and should bring to their knowledge all things whatsoever he had said to them. So that in their teaching and in their living they might mistake in no respect. What, therefore, these men taught and what they did, both directly and indirectly, become to us a guide in our Christian service.

Many things which the Savior taught the apostles were not reported in the gospels. Many years after the Lord had ascended into the heavens, we hear Paul mention a saying of the Master, which was commonly understood by all disciples at that time: "It is more blessed to give than to receive." Acts 20:35. This was not only a teaching of the Lord, but it was one of those common sayings of his of which every one had heard. And yet no report of it had come down to them by means of the writings of the evangelists.

Not only many things were said by the Lord during his earthly ministry that found no place in the four gospels, but he did many things which were never reported by these writers. John supposes that if they had given an itemized account of all that he did, that the world would not contain the books.

Hence, it is evident to any one who wishes to learn of God's will concerning us, that we must necessarily wait upon the apostles in order that we may know the Lord's will concerning the conduct of his disciples.

They try to find fault with this, sometimes, and urge that a covenant must all have been put to record before the covenant-sealing act, and that after the sacrifice by which it is sanctified, has been made, nothing can be added thereto. In this calculation they commit several blunders. I will name them in the order in which they occur to me:

1st. They take for granted that everything in connection with the sacrifice of Christ must be in the precise order in which they have found covenants and sacrifices at all other times. And yet the very first feature of this service is irregular. The passover, which had always been regarded as a type of the offering of Christ for us, required, first, the slaying of the lamb, and after that the covenant meal. This had been the manner of ratifying covenants in all the ages, or of renewing them. But Jesus ate the passover before he was crucified, indeed, before the time for the eating of the passover had come. And in the conclusion of that solemn service, he took bread and blessed and brake and gave unto them, telling them, "This is my body," and then he took the cup, and said, "This is my blood of the New Covenant, shed for many, for the remission of sins." And yet, at that time, his body had not been bruised, nor had his blood been shed. Of course, this is out of the order of all covenant making. But when we have the facts recorded, and know that this was the order of that New Institution, it is better for us to accept it than to reject it because of something which we have denominated an irregularity.

2d. They take it for granted that all the teaching and requirements of a covenant must first be made known before it could be ratified by sacrifice or meal. This is a great mistake. The covenant of Exodus was ratified by sacrifice and meal when the people knew but little of the terms upon which they were to have their liberty. They were not aware of the route over which they were to travel, of the hunger and thirst which were to follow, nor of the law under which they were to live in order to inherit the promised land. These features of the covenant were to follow. Nor was the Levitical law given when it was ratified in covenant. When Moses took the book and sprinkled it, as well as the people, in the solemnization of the covenant which God then made with that people, it contained nothing but the merest epitome of the law under which they were to live and to which they then bound themselves. This covenant was forty years in its completion. And yet it was as binding on them as if it had been given in one day.

3d. They urge that everything which Jesus had intended his disciples to do, had been taught before his death. And yet he told them that there were many things which he could not teach them then because they could not comprehend them. Hence, just as it was in giving the Old Covenant to the Children of Israel, they received the instruction as they became competent to understand it. The truth, in both cases, was that they bound themselves to whatever God required them to do. And yet they did not know all that would be imposed upon them. At the time that Christ made and sealed his Covenant there was nothing written. It was many years after this when the gospels made their appearance. And yet to deny that he made a Covenant with his people is to deny the plain statement of the word of God.

4th. And yet, for all we can know to the contrary, every feature of the New Institution had been given to the apostles before Christ suffered on the cross. Still they might need the further instruction of the Holy Spirit, to enable them to comprehend it and to teach it infallibly to others.

Hence, when they object to anything as belonging to the Covenant of Christ, except those things which had been clearly stated as having been given before, they do so without any scriptural reasons whatever.

This leaves us not only to the direct statements found in the gospels, but to the teachings found in the Acts of the Apostles, and in the Epistolary communications of these inspired men. But much of the teaching found in the Acts of the Apostles is in action. I do not mean by this that these men made no mistakes in their conduct. I do not justify Peter in dissembling at Antioch, nor do I suppose that Paul and Barnabas were both right in their opinions concerning the propriety of taking with them John Mark on their proposed second missionary tour. What we mean is this, the action of these men, and of the churches under their teaching, having the silent approval of themselves and co-laborers, is a guide to us, as much as what they commanded.

With those who are something more than mere quibblers, who have a hobby to be sustained by mere technicalities, the question is, what would God have me to do? And understanding what inspired men regarded as their duty and the duty of the church at that time, we feel that, if we do the same things now, we shall be doing the will of God. We may put this in the form of a syllogism, thus: (1) Those men did the will of God. (2) That will has not been changed from that time to this. (3) Therefore, if we do the same things now, we will be doing the will of God.

With this rule before us, we will try to find just what they did and taught that we may know just what God would have us to do now. If the church under the teaching of the apostles kept the Sabbath, that will be sufficient reason why we should keep it. If they did not keep it as a sacred day, and if they told us that we are free from the law of which it was a part, and, therefore, that no man has any right to judge us in any matter of this kind, we feel at liberty to follow that teaching. We have seen this already. But we are now to see if they regarded any day as sacred, and if so, which of the seven.

It will not be necessary for us to find them saying that the first day of the week is a sacred day; if they so devoted the day it is enough.

CHAPTER II.

THE VIEW ENTERTAINED BY CHRISTIANS IN GENERAL.

Adventists generally discard this as evidence. They tell us that these views have been wrong, and that the whole question must be settled by the word of God and by that alone. "And that to insist on any testimony from the religious world, will be to lay the foundations for apostasy." By such evidence, they say, "we could sustain infant baptism, or sprinkling, instead of the immersion which Jesus taught, or any of the forms of merely human origin."

And yet when they can find the religious world blending the law and the gospel, and urging their memberships to keep the Sabbath, they are not slow to remind us of the fact that they hold the same opinion which the great men have always held, and, therefore, there is strong reason for regarding their views in that respect, as being well sustained. With them, it depends somewhat upon whose ox is being gored. If I should do the same thing with this human testimony which they do, they should not grumble.

It should be remembered, however, that while testimony of this kind can serve in no sense to set aside the statements of the word of God, or to sustain customs for which nothing was ever claimed by way of divine appointment, still, respecting those questions in which men have examined the word of God and founded their practice on what they have, in this way, come to regard as the requirements of heaven; and, especially, in those matters where there has been perfect unanimity of sentiment, such views are worthy of the highest respect.

If our question related to a matter in which religious people are to be found keeping a law or a custom under which they had been raised, the testimony would certainly amount to but very little. All prejudices and customs are in favor of those things with which we have been familiar. Such things might continue for centuries, without any one taking the trouble to investigate the question in any way. It is easy to retain the customs of the past, but very difficult to remove them. Hence, in any case where we find a large number of people ceasing from any former religious custom, we may be pretty well assured of one or two things: either the change is being made for convenience's sake, to something which will satisfy conscience, and yet is very much more easily practiced, than what was formerly done, or they are making the change from conviction of right.

Concerning the keeping of a day, there would be nothing to be gained in the way of ease. It would be as difficult to observe the first day of the week as to keep the seventh. Indeed, it would be much more difficult. They were surrounded by Jews in the early times, and from these the change comes. To act in harmony with their customs would be comparatively easy, while to change the custom in this respect would be attended with a great deal of annoyance. Nor was this all: their own prejudices were in the way. These early Christians had been Jews, and would naturally feel inclined to retain as much of their old religion as possible. Many of them had the idea that the Gentiles had no right to be saved. And even when they became convinced that they were to be accepted as well as the Jews, they thought that they must be circumcised and keep the law of Moses, or they could not be saved. The apostles knew better, but they met the prejudice of the whole church at this point. Now, for this people to change from the seventh to the first day of the week, declares that, in their minds, there were sound scriptural reasons for doing so.

And still further: the religious world has had the prejudice of a mistaken interpretation to contend with upon this point during all these centuries.

At a very early period in the history of the church, the desire was manifested to accommodate the religion of Christ to the tastes and customs of the world. Rather than to offend the Jew who was zealous for the law, they were ready to yield to his demands, either in practice or in theory. In this way they accommodated Christianity to the Gentile world. And many of the forms and ceremonies of the Catholic Church to-day are nothing but baptized heathenisms. Also, many other things are a mixture of Paganism and Judaism. And, like many of the reformatory kings in Israel, who tried to remove idolatry without removing the idols or stopping the worship in the high places, our reformers have handed down to us a large number of customs and doctrines labeled "Christianity" that were received from the Mother Church. Because of this desire to accommodate the religion of Christ to the wish of the Jews, they have entertained the idea that Christians are now keeping the law of Moses. In this way they talk and teach of baptism in the room of circumcision, and of keeping the Sabbath when they are only keeping the first day of the week. But with this feeling in the mind that we are under the law, there has been, during the ages, all the pleading which has ever been made for a scriptural practice, to return to the keeping of the seventh day of the week. Certainly nothing has kept them from returning to that law in practice as well as in theory, but the fact that they could not find that the apostles and early Christians did so.

Then we find that this change has not only taken place, but that it has come in opposition to all the prejudices of the people who made it and of those who have continued it.

Indeed, we shall hereafter find that zealots for the law kept both days. They regarded the seventh day because of the decalogue, and observed the first day of the week because of the practice of the apostles and the first Christians.

The Ebionites, as related by Theodoret, held this view and kept both days. Dr. Moses Stuart, of Andover, says, referring to that statement of Theodoret: "This gives a good historical view of the state of things in the early ages of the church. The zealots for the law wished the Jewish Sabbath to be observed as well as the Lord's day; for about the latter, there appears never to have been any question among any class of Christians, so far as I have been able to discover. The early Christians, one and all of them, held the first day of the week to be sacred."

Does some one say that even so learned a man as Dr. Stuart might have been mistaken? We do not claim infallibility for him. And yet to say that he was as familiar with all the customs of past ages, and especially with those which related to the religion of Christ, as any man whose name is known to the reading public, and that he would be as conscientious in stating these facts as any to whom reference might be made, is only to state truth in a very feeble way. He was a prince of scholars; a man of pains-taking, carefulness and accuracy in all he said and wrote. Such testimony must have great weight with those who are wishing for light respecting the views and practices of Christians from the very first.

I am not aware that this statement of the Professor has ever been seriously questioned by any one. So far as I know, both parties accept his statement as being, at least, substantially correct. This gives us the assistance of a strong argument; one that is not to be lightly thrown aside.

We have as many quotations at hand as it would be possible to use in a work of reasonable limits, showing that the unanimous opinion of the whole church has been, from the very first, that the Lord's day, or the first day of the week, should be observed as a sacred day by all Christians. But for the present, we want to go a step further, and show the purpose had in view in meeting together. It would be too much to say that all disciples of Jesus have ever been agreed in this purpose, for not all have studied the subject. But I shall quote the opinions of those who are most entitled to consideration, showing that, in their view of the matter, the chief purpose for these meetings on the first day of the week was to break bread, or attend to the communion.

William King, Archbishop of Dublin, in a sermon concerning the "*inventions of men in the worship of God*," says:

"It is manifest that if it be not our own faults, we may have an opportunity every Lord's day when we meet together; and, therefore, that church is guilty of laying aside the command, whose order and worship doth not require and provide for this practice. Christ's command seems to lead us directly to it: for, 'Do this in remembrance of me,' implies that Christ was to leave them, that they were to meet together after he was gone, and that he required them to remember him at their meetings whilst he was absent. The very design of our public meetings on the Lord's day, *not on the Jewish Sabbath*, is to remember and keep in our minds a sense of what Christ did and suffered for us till he come again; and this we are obliged to do, not in such a manner as our own inventions suggest, but by such means as Christ himself has prescribed to us, that is, by celebrating this holy ordinance.

"It seems, then, probable, from the very institution of this ordinance, that our Savior designed it should be a part of God's service, in all the solemn assemblies of Christians, as the passover was in the assemblies of the Jews. To know, therefore, how often Christ requires us to celebrate this feast, we have no more to do, but to inquire how often Christ requires us to meet together; that is, at least every Lord's day."

Dr. Scott, in his commentary on Acts 20:7, says: "*Breaking of bread*, or, commemorating the death of Christ in the eucharist, was one chief end of their assembling; this ordinance seems to have been constantly administered every Lord's day, and probably no professed Christians absented themselves from it, after they had been admitted into the church; unless they lay under some censure, or had some real hindrance."

Dr. Mason, in his "Lectures on Frequent Communion," Edinburgh edition, says: "Communion every Lord's day was universal, and was preserved in the Greek church till the seventh century; and such as neglected three weeks together were excommunicated."

John Wesley, in a letter to America, 1784, said: "I, also, advise the elders to administer the supper of the Lord on every Lord's day."

In all the ages of the church there have been a large number of devout men demanding that the church should return to what they denominate the practice of the apostles respecting the communion, that of meeting together on every first day of the week to remember the Lord's death in that Institution, till he shall come again.

Dr. Barnes makes this note on Acts 20:7: "*And upon the first day of the week.* Showing thus that this day was then observed by Christians as holy time. Comp. 1 Cor. 16:2; Rev. 1:10. *To break bread.* Evidently to celebrate the Lord's Supper. Comp. chap. 2:46. So the Syriac understands it, by translating it, ' to break the eucharist '; that is the eucharistic bread. It is probable that the apostles and early Christians celebrated the Lord's Supper on every Lord's day."

There is so much of candor in this that it is surely entitled to consideration. The practice of the church to which Dr. Barnes belonged was in the way of this clear acknowledgment. Still he makes it, because it seemed to him as the evident teaching of the Scriptures on the subject.

In the *Encyclopedia Britannica,* under the head of "*Eucharist,*" we have this statement: "With regard to the frequency of Holy Communion, although it has been concluded with much probability from Acts 2:46 that the earliest Christians, in the first fervor of their faith, partook of the Eucharist daily, appearances are rather in favor of a weekly celebration on the Lord's day being the rule in the apostolic and primitive church. It was on the 'first day of the week' that the Christians met for breaking bread at Troas (Acts 20:7); and St. Paul's direction to the Corinthian Christians to lay by for the poor on that day, may be reasonably associated with the oblations at the time of celebration. Pliny tells us that it was on a 'fixed day, *stato die,* the Christians came together for prayer and communion,' and, as we have seen, Justin Martyr speaks of Sunday by name (*hee legomenee heliou hemera*) as the day of celebration."

From chapter fourteen of the "*Teaching of the Twelve Apostles*" we have the following, as their instruction respecting the communion:

"And every Lord's day, having gathered yourselves together, ye shall break bread and give thanks, having moreover confessed your transgressions, in order that your sacrifice may be pure."

It is not proper to make the claim that some have made for this manuscript, that it was not more than fifty years on this side of the Apostle John. We do know, however, that Justin taught as plainly as that, at still an earlier day, though he used the Roman term "Sunday" instead of Lord's day, as found in this writing. But it is safe to say that the manuscript was of very early date, and tells very clearly how early Christians understood this service.

We are greatly tempted to give a number of such quotations from Christian workers and thinkers during the ages, but we must not take the space to do so. Rev. C. H. Spurgeon now communes on every recurring Lord's day, and in the minds of the great host of Christian thinkers it was the primitive custom. And there remains no room for doubt that when the religious world shall come to look upon apostolic precedent as a proper guide for all Christians in all time, the whole church will return to this ancient custom.

CHAPTER III.

UNFAIR METHODS OF ADVANCING THE CAUSE OF THE SABBATH, AND OF OPPOSING THE LORD'S DAY.

I. Adventists usually take advantage of the desire of the people for something new. There are hundreds of Athenians yet in the world, who spend their time in nothing else than to tell or hear of something new. Such persons are able to find that many things which we now know to be true were once denied. The conservative forces have many times been in the wrong. Hence, they jump to the conclusion that, in all matters in which some new theory is opposed, the opposition must necessarily be wrong, and the novel doctrine right. About all, therefore, necessary to be done to carry any cause in the minds of such persons, is to convince them that the doctrine in question is new; that it is feared and avoided by many who are unwilling to accept any change, and they at once accept the novel position as being correct. Of course such persons are not of much account to them or anybody else; they will change that for something else as soon as the tide shall run some other way. They are light clouds having no water, and are, therefore, carried about with every wind of doctrine. But they count. The piety of this class rarely becomes more than a hobby-riding zeal. But there is an evidence of success in the addition of numbers. And in the newness of zeal and in the enjoyment of the new fellowship, they are willing to be tithed. While they do not sustain the cause in that locality, their contributions carry the work into some other community where there may be found other people like themselves who are willing to assist for a time, and in that way the cause is kept moving.

II. Advent preachers usually light upon some undefended community. They find some place where the sectarianism of the times has so divided and weakened the churches that no one party is able to have preaching but a small part of the time, and this not by the ablest men. These communities are not in communication with those who can defend the doctrine of the Scriptures respecting this Institution, and they would not be able to obtain his service for the want of means. Here the Adventists find a good field, and are able to get the people to commit themselves in a covenant to keep the Sabbath before any defense of the gospel can be had. A discussion, if one obtains at all, is usually after they have succeeded in fastening the masses to their opinions, when it is not easy to change the current after the recent shower.

A mistake is generally committed, too, by the friends of the truth, in saying: "Let them alone, they will come to naught themselves." No doubt that the storm will pass by, and that a calm will follow. But how much timber will be destroyed is another question. As the prick of a needle in the spinal marrow of the child may make a hunch-back for life, so by these views here lodged in the souls of the young of that community, their religion is maimed forever. If these men could always be met by the proper means at the right time, they would never do any lasting damage to any people. But from a false policy, a divided Christianity, or from indifference, the work of ruin is not checked.

III. *Everything is turned into persecution.* They come into town and continue a meeting for one or two months, during that time they challenge the people in one way or another fifty times for an investigation. But if some one proposes to investigate, they raise the cry of persecution. They claim to have been peaceably preaching what they believe, and that some one is disturbing them. They learned this of the Mormons, from whom Mrs. White, their Prophetess, learned to have revelations. This has been their mode of claiming the sympathy, and begging the toleration of an injured people.

IV. Many honest and intelligent people are deceived by the statements of history which they have published. I know of no work more deserving of censure for unfairness than "The History of the Sabbath," by J. N. Andrews. Scraps of statements are taken out of their legitimate connections, and testimonies wrung from authors who testified nothing in their favor. To call such procedure pettifogging, is to apply a term entirely too feeble for the expression of the true thought. He has not only quoted every erratic statement which could be so applied as to favor his theory, but he finds history which other men can not find. In the second edition of the work the author acknowledges to have quoted from an edition of Neander not now in use, and to have used a statement which the historian did not put into his revised work. Many Sabbatarians have been found in the different ages of the church. Of course these can be had to testify in favor of that institution. After the year 585, the church of Rome combined the Sabbath with the Lord's day, or taught that the Lord's day was given to take the place of the Sabbath. Hence, since that time it has been common to speak of the Lord's day as the Sabbath. Many writers have spoken of the Institution by that term, and Sabbatarians commonly take advantage of the fact to make it appear that the author was testifying to their institution, the seventh day.

V. It is common, I might say universal, to claim that Sunday had no existence till the time of Constantine, or that it was never regarded as sacred till that time, and then only by virtue of the edict of a king who was a heathen. If you hear a lecture from one of them it will be clearly affirmed; if you read a tract, it will be boldly stated, but if you have before you a work which is expected to fall into the way of the critical world, you will find it only hinted. After the patched work of quotations has been furnished, the author will assume such to be the purport of what has been produced. As a sample of many things which might be cited, I call attention to Mr. Andrews on the Sabbath, pp. 346-7:

"On the seventh day of March, (321,) Constantine published his edict commanding the observance of that ancient festival of the heathen, the venerable day of the sun. On the following day, March eighth, he issued a second decree in every respect worthy of its heathen predecessor. The purport of it was this: 'That if any royal edifice should be struck by lightning, the ancient ceremonies of propitiating the Deity should be practiced, and the *haruspices* should be consulted to learn the meaning of the awful portent. The *haruspices* were soothsayers who foretold future events by examining the entrails of beasts slaughtered in sacrifice to the gods. The statute of the seventh of March enjoining the observance of the venerable day of the sun, and that of the eighth of the same month commanding the consultation of the *haruspices*, constitute a noble pair of well-matched heathen edicts. That Constantine, himself, was a heathen at the time these edicts were issued, is shown not only by the nature of the edicts themselves, but by the fact that his nominal conversion to Christianity is placed by Mosheim two years after his Sunday law.'"

This is the manner of the argument. What is lacking in the testimony is to be made up by telling the readers what is the sum or the purport of an edict. I have no interest in defending Constantine. He exhibited many inconsistencies. He was a politician, and, while he came eventually to regard Christianity as the only religion which could be of any particular value to any person, and though we could not say that he had reached that conclusion in the year 321, we must say, if we have paid any attention to the edict itself, that it was his purpose to set Christians at liberty to worship as they preferred. This, however, was not all; he extended the same rights to all his subjects. As to his requiring any day to be kept as a day of heathen worship, there is not a particle of evidence in its favor. History can not even be distorted into such a thought. No Christian understood it so, and if that had been the idea which attached to that edict, Christians would not have submitted. They were yet ready to die for their faith in Christ, and would not, under any circumstances, have submitted to a heathen worship. But instead of that, they regarded it as a release for their religion and a restoration of their liberties.

Nothing more than disgust can be excited for the shallow pretensions or utter disregard for truth of a man who will say that Constantine wished to favor heathenism by the so-called Sunday law of 321. From 313 he had been removing all obstructions to Christian worship, and those who were in slavery were released. Those who had lost their lands had them restored to them again. He even went so far as to urge his people to accept of this religion. Hence no man can find an easier way of convincing all readers of history of his entire unworthiness as an author than to make such statements respecting Constantine and his edicts as are made by Mr. Andrews.

In Smith's Dictionary of the Bible, Am. ed., under the "*Lord's day*," I find the following very sensible view of the whole matter as it relates to Constantine:

"4th. That Constantine then instituted Sunday for the first time as a religious day for Christians.

"The fourth of these statements is absolutely refuted, both by the quotations made above from writers of the second and third centuries, and by the terms of the edict itself. It is evident that Constantine, accepting as facts the existence of the *Solis Dies*, and the reverence paid to it by some one or other, does nothing more than make that reverence practically universal. It is '*venerabilis*' already. And it is probable that this most natural interpretation would never have been disturbed, had not Sozomen asserted, without warrant from either Justinian or Theodosian code, that Constantine did for the sixth day of the week what the codes assert he did for the first. . . . .

"It is a fact, that in the year A. D. 321, in a public edict which was to apply to Christians as well as to Pagans, he put especial honor upon a day already honored by the former, judicially calling it by a name which Christians had long employed without scruple, and to which, as it was in ordinary use, the Pagans could scarcely object. What he did for it was to insist that worldly business, whether by the functionaries of the law or by private citizens, should be intermitted during its continuance. An exception indeed was made in favor of the rural districts, avowedly from the necessity of the case, covertly, perhaps, to prevent those districts, where Paganism (as the word Pagus would intimate) still prevailed extensively, from feeling aggrieved by a sudden and stringent change. It need only be added here that the readiness with which Christians acquiesced in the interdiction of business on the Lord's day, affords no small presumption that they had long considered it to be a day of rest, and that, so far as circumstances admitted, they had made it so long before.

"Were any other testimony wanting to the existence of Sunday as a day of Christian worship at this period, it might be supplied by the Council of Nicea, A. D. 325. The fathers there and then assembled make no doubt of the obligation of that day—do not ordain it—do not defend it. They assume it as an existing fact, and only notice it incidentally in order to regulate an indifferent matter, the posture of Christian worship on it.

"Richard Baxter has well summed up the history of the Lord's day at this point, and his words may not be inaptly inserted here: 'That the first Christian emperor, finding all Christians in the unanimous possession of the day, should make a law (as our kings do) for the due observance of it, and that the Christian Council should establish uniformity in the very gesture of worship on that day, are strong confirmations of the matter of fact, that the churches unanimously agreed in the holy use of it, as a separated day even from and in the apostles' days.' *Richard Baxter on the Divine Appointment of the Lord's day, p. 41.*"

This is rather a long quotation, but it is so directly to the point that it seemed best to give it in its connection. I could quote from almost any number of good authors, showing that the use made of the edict of Constantine by Mr. Andrews is unjust and unreasonable. I do not know of any historian who will agree with his use of that edict. It is not only unfair and unreasonable, but it shows that the mind of the gentleman is greatly warped by his particular views of theology.

In Blackburn's Church History, page 70, the author says.

"The edicts of Constantine from 312 to 325 show an ecclesiastical spirit. They refer largely to the building and repair of churches, and liberal gifts to them; the restoration of property of Christians, who must be equally just to the Pagans; mutual toleration of religions; the settlement of religious disputes; the calling of local councils; the exemption of the clergy from civil offices and taxes; the burning of Jews who should assail Christians; the emancipation of slaves; the general observance of Sunday (*solis dies*); restoration of property to the heirs of martyrs; careful provision for the poor; the release of Christians from the mines; the forbidding of images—even his own statue must not be set up in the temples; severe penalties upon heathen diviners and priests who should perform sacrifices in private houses, and practice magic; and the earnest advice that all his subjects adopt Christianity."

Remark would seem to be unnecessary. It must be evident that if Mr. Andrews is right in his use of the edict of Constantine there is nothing to be gained by reading history.

Two very distinct views are entertained respecting Constantine. One is that he was a saint. This comes from the services which he rendered the church, and the extravagant views of Eusebius of Nicomedia, who baptized him, a short time before his death. A truer judgment is, however, generally indulged; that he was an ambitious statesman, who had knowledge of the innocence of those Christians who had suffered severely at the hands of the Pagans, and that he aimed to redress them; that he knew that this religion was for the good of the nation, and hence, that in rendering it any real service, he would advance his people in the elements of refinement and prosperity; and that in using the *solis dies* he only employed a term which was already in existence, and which was known to refer to the first day of the week. That heathens may have observed this day, has nothing to do with the edict, nor its purpose.

VI. Adventists insinuate that the Lord's day is a creation of the Catholic Church; that it came into existence as many other customs of purely human origin.

That this position is quite antagonistic to the one just mentioned, namely, that it was of heathen origin, does not seem to disconcert them in the least. I will cite one quotation as a sample of many which might be given.

Hist. Sab. Andrews, p. 228 : " The Lord's day of the Catholic Church can be traced no nearer to John than A. D. 194, or perhaps, in strict truth, to A. D. 200, and those who then use the name show plainly that they did not believe it to be the Lord's day by apostolic appointment. To hide these fatal facts by seeming to trace the title back to Ignatius, a disciple of John, and thus to identify Sunday with the Lord's day of that apostle, a series of remarkable frauds have been committed which we have had occasion to examine."

Now, this is the most remarkable statement that I ever saw in a religious book. Indeed, the quotations he has made himself, prove his statement perfectly untrue. I know no way to account for such rash utterances but to suppose the man to have been exceedingly mad against the first day of the week, and, therefore, willing to go to any length to *find* something or *make it*, that would show the Lord's day in a bad light.

I think some Catholic priest can be found somewhere who will claim that his church changed that day. I think I remember having seen that claim set up, and Acts xx: 7, referred to as proof. And yet every reader of history knows that from the very days of the apostles the first day of the week has been observed as a day of worship. It is known, too, that the church was quite free from anything that would entitle it to such designations as Catholic, (in the sense of Roman Catholic,) for several hundred years. To show how perfectly unreliable Mr. A. is concerning facts, and consistency both, I will give the quotation he makes from Mosheim, and that, too, on the very next page to that from which I have quoted already. Let it be remembered that Mosheim is writing of the first century, and telling of customs which existed before John was dead, indeed, before he was cast away upon the Isle of Patmos.

"All Christians were unanimous in setting apart the first day of the week, on which the triumphant Savior rose from the dead, for the solemn celebration of public worship. This pious custom, which was derived from the example of the church of Jerusalem, was founded upon the express appointment of the apostles, who consecrated that day to the same sacred purpose, and was observed universally throughout the Christian churches, as appears from the united testimony of the most credible writers."

Now what can be said of the consistency, say nothing of the veracity, of a man who, with this language staring him in the face, can muster the courage to say that the Lord's day (which we know refers to the first day of the week, in the language of the Catholics) can not be traced nearer to John than A. D. 194. When he was writing the statement he knew that the very best historical authority which can be found traces that observance to the first century, and finds it even before the death of that apostle. Nor is this all, Mr. A. has given the statements of the most reliable historians to the effect that the first day of the week, or Lord's day, or Sunday, was religiously observed all the way from the apostles down to the time he says it may first be found. Why, then, he chooses to fly in his own face and contradict himself, as well as all reliable history, is a most difficult question. Does he mean to discredit history, and simply quote those men to show what fools they have made of themselves? or does his Judaism really interfere with his sanity?

VII. *Adventists constantly play upon words.* Find the ancients observing Lord's day, and so affirming, then it does not mean the first day of the week, but the day of the Lord's Judgment, or it must mean the Sabbath, which, in the Old Testament, was regarded as "My holy day." There may be every evidence of the sense in which the author employes the term, but that must pass for nothing. To be able to quibble out of its evident import seems to be the only aim.

If Justin Martyr spoke of the first day of the week by the term Sunday, then it must count for nothing: it is a heathen word. If the first day of the week is spoken of as a day of Christian gathering, then it was for some other purpose than the worship of God. If they are spoken of as meeting on that day for the purpose of breaking bread, then it was an accident, or a mere incident, and can have nothing to do with giving the practice of the people. And when they can find nothing else to say, they demand that somewhere it ought to be found that the Savior commanded his apostles to observe the first day of the week as a sacred day. I presume if this could be found, it would be said: "Yes, it was a sacred day, and so are all days sacred to the Lord."

If they find anywhere that the word "*festival*" has been used in connection with the Lord's day or Sunday, then it is proof that it was only a day of recreation, and in no sense a day of worship. Though it be found that they did act unadvisedly in respect of festivities on that day, and some man can be found saying that these *Sunday festivities* were only a human institution, it must be found that he means that Sunday is a human institution! Though if the language was submitted to any class in rhetoric or logic in the country, the unanimous decision would be that the author meant to say that it was the unscriptural use of the day, and not the day itself, that was condemned as a human institution, still, as they can clip the quotation and retain a jingle of words suitable to their purpose, they are willing to sacrifice the evident meaning of the language, that a hobby may be sustained.

CHAPTER IV.

HISTORY SHOWS THAT THE LORD'S DAY, OR FIRST DAY OF THE WEEK, HAS BEEN REGARDED AS A SACRED DAY IN ALL AGES OF THE CHURCH.

I begin with a statement of the opinion of the teachings of history on this subject, by B. B. Edwards, in his " Encyclopedia of Religious Knowledge," published 1858, found on page 1,040 :

" We are informed by Eusebius that from the beginning the Christians assembled on the first day of the week, called by them the Lord's day, for the purpose of religious worship, to read the Scriptures, to preach and to celebrate the Lord's Supper."

Now, we are not ready to say that the author has misunderstood his reading, nor that Eusebius has been untrue to the facts in the case. And unless we may impeach one or the other of these witnesses, the question is put to rest with this statement.

" Chamber's Encyclopedia " has the following on the subject of the Sabbath :

He has come to the edict of Constantine, and gives us something on this side of it: " A new era in the history of the Lord's day now commenced ; tendencies toward Sabbatarianism, or confusion of the Christian with the Jewish Institution beginning to manifest themselves. These were slight till the end of the 5th century, and are traceable chiefly to the evils of legislation."

" Johnson's Encyclopedia " has this to say on the subject of the Sabbath :

" The resurrection of Christ and his subsequent appearances to his disciples till his ascension, and the miraculous descent of the Holy Spirit on the first day of the week, led to that being set apart for the special religious assemblies of the Christians, and for the simple services of their faith. For a time the Jewish converts observed both the seventh day, to which the name Sabbath continued to be given exclusively, and the first day, which came to be called Lord's day. Later, the Apostle

Paul sought to relieve their consciences from the obligations of keeping the Sabbath (Rom. 14:5; Col. 2 16). . . . . Within a century after the death of the last of the apostles we find the observance of the first day of the week, under the name of the Lord's day, established as an universal custom of the church, according to the unanimous testimony of Barnabas, Ignatius, Pliny, Justin Martyr, and Tertullian. It was regarded not as a continuation of the Jewish Sabbath (which was denounced together with circumcision and other Jewish anti-Christian practices), but rather as a substitute for it; and naturally its observance was based on the resurrection of Christ rather than on the creation rest-day or the Sabbath of the Decalogue."

As to the origin of the word Sunday, there seems to be no settled view, but some things are agreed to universally, that it was the first day of the week, and that at an early date it came to be used as a synonym for Lord's day.

With this thought before us we are prepared to hear Mosheim as translated by Murdock, Vol. 1, p. 137, say of the practice of the second century: "When the Christians celebrated the Lord's Supper, which they were accustomed to do chiefly on Sundays, they consecrated a part of the bread and wine of the oblations by certain prayers pronounced by the president, the bishop of the congregation."

Same book, p. 278, sec. 5, Mosheim says: "The first day of the week, (on which Christians were accustomed to meet for the worship of God,) Constantine required, by a special law, to be observed more sacredly than before."

Once more from the same work: Century II., Part II., Chap, iv., section 8: "The Christians assembled for the worship of God in private dwelling-houses, in caves, and places where the dead were buried. They met on the first day of the week; and here and there also on the seventh day, which was the Jewish Sabbath."

Then again, in Book I., Century I., Part II., Chap. iv., Sec. 4: "The Christians of this century assembled for the worship of God and for the advancement of their own piety on the first day of the week, the day on which Christ re-assumed his life; for that this day was set apart for religious worship by the apostles themselves, and that, after the manner of the church at Jerusalem, it was generally observed, we have unexceptionable testimony. Moreover, those congregations which either lived intermingled with Jews, or were composed in great measure of Jews, were accustomed to observe also the seventh day of the week, as a sacred day: for doing which the other Christians taxed them with no wrong."

Now, so far as history is concerned, we have traced the keeping of the first day of the week, or Sunday, or Lord's day, back through the fourth century, the third, the second, and away down into the first; right up to the apostles who were at Jerusalem. Not only so, but we have used their own author, or at least the favored translation of Mosheim.

He finds those Judaizers there just as Paul and Silas did, only Mosheim notices those who were less determined in their plans and methods of worship. Those of whom Luke speaks taught that unless the Gentiles were circumcised and would keep the law they could not be saved. But those our historian speaks of kept the first day of the week and also the seventh. The other Christians only kept the first day of the week.

It would seem unreasonable that we should quote another line of history, for if what we have seen will not convince a man that Christians have kept the first day of the week as a sacred day in all ages of the church, then to such a man history can have but little influence. Still I am disposed to go further and let other historians and commentators and critics have their say on the subject. I do this for two reasons: first, because these witnesses have been badly dealt with, and, secondly, because they throw light on the meaning of many Scriptures, that are not understood by many persons, simply because the manner of speech differs from ours.

J. N. Andrews, Hist. Sabbath, p. 229, 230, says: "Now let us read what Neander, the most distinguished of church historians, says of this apostolic authority for Sunday observance: 'The festival of Sunday, like all other festivals, was always only a human ordinance, and it was far from the intentions of the apostles to establish a divine command in this respect; far from them and from the early apostolic church, to transfer the laws of the Sabbath to Sunday. Perhaps at the end of the second century a false application of this kind had begun to take place; for men appear by that time to have considered laboring on Sunday as a sin."

This language Mr. Andrews cites to rebut the testimony of Mosheim, whom we have already quoted, showing that the first day of the week was observed from the very first as a day of worship. Now, while this quotation was left out of Neander in its reproduction, I must say that I see nothing damaging in it. If the author had before his mind the first day of the week, and was trying to show that its observance was not apostolic, still it would have been simply the opinion of that man as against ten thousand men equally critical in exegesis. But he had before him a wrong use of that day in establishing a feast on that occasion. It was the festival of Sunday that he condemned. And that is the same thing that Paul condemned in the church at Corinth: not the day on which they met, but the *festival* on that day. The author further shows that the early Christians did not regard Sunday as being Sabbath. This, again, is certainly correct.

But Mr. Andrews relieves us of any further trouble about the missing quotation. He says:

"It is true that in re-writing his work he omitted this sentence. But he inserted nothing of a contrary character, and the general tenor of the revised edition is in this place precisely the same as in that from which this out-spoken statement is taken."

And then to prove that Neander held the same views in the later work he quotes from vol. 1, p. 295, Torrey's translation: "Sunday was distinguished as a day of joy, by being exempted from fasts, and by the circumstance that prayer was performed on this day in a standing and not in a kneeling posture, as Christ by his resurrection, has raised up fallen man again to heaven."

Now, what is there in this that condemns Sunday observance? The historian only shows that the early Christians met together on that day and were glad in view of the resurrection of the Lord from the dead. While this may not, in any way, conflict with the quotation which is now acknowledged to be missing, it would antagonize it very strongly if the meaning of the former was that of condemning the Sunday as not apostolic. Hence, we know that his wonderful quotation, with which he sought to make Neander oppose Mosheim, had no such meaning as that which he gave it.

But I am not done yet with Neander. In his "*Planting and Training of the Christian Church,*" a work devoted exclusively to the first century, page 159, he says :

"But since we are not authorized to make this assumption, unless a church consisted for the most part of those who had been Jewish proselytes, we shall be compelled to conclude that the religious observances of Sunday occasioned its being considered the first day of the week. It is also mentioned in Acts 20 : 7, that the church at Troas assembled on Sunday and celebrated the Lord's Supper."

Again, same page :

"They rejected the Sabbath which the Jewish Christians celebrated, in order to avoid the risk of mingling Judaism and Christianity, and because another event associated more closely another day with their feelings. For, since the sufferings and resurrection of Christ appeared as the central point of Christian knowledge and practice ; since his resurrection was viewed as the foundation of all Christian joy and hope, it was natural that the day which was connected with the remembrance of this event, should be specially devoted to Christian communion."

Now, if this does not show that Neander was of the opinion that the early Christians regarded the first day of the week as a sacred day, then language can not be so constructed as to present that thought.

But to turn to the very volume from which Mr. Andrews makes his quotation, to show that Neander, in his new work, agrees with his distortion of what he claimed to have found in a former work, and on the same page, only a few sentences from the one to which Mr. A. refers, we read : (See Vol. I., p. 295).

"The opposition to Judaism early led to the special observance of Sunday in the place of the Sabbath. The first intimation of this is in Acts xx : 7, where we find the church assembled on the first day of the week ; a still later one is in Rev. 1 : 10, where, by the Lord's day can hardly be understood the day of judgment. As the Sabbath was regarded as representing Judaism, Sunday was contemplated as a symbol of the new life consecrated to the risen Christ and grounded in his resurrection. Sunday was distinguished as a day of joy."

With all these facts before me, and knowing that they were before Mr. Andrews, it is a strain on my charity to not think of him as deliberately falsifying history. Neander uses the three words, Sunday, first day, and Lord's day as expressive of the same occasion: they all and severally mean the resurrection day, were so regarded by early Christians, and the day was kept as a sacred day, a day in which Christians were to meet, and engage in communion. Again on page 332 of this same volume we have the following:

"As we have already remarked, celebration of the Lord's Supper was still held to constitute an essential part of divine worship on every Sunday, as appears from Justin Martyr; and the whole church partook of the communion after they had joined in the amen of the preceding prayer."

So much for Neander. He teaches as positively the opposite of what Mr. Andrews represents him as teaching as it would be possible for one man to differ from the teaching of another.

One more specimen of the unfairness of Mr. Andrews. He quotes from Tertullian, who wrote towards the close of the second century. The first is from Tertullian on Prayer, Chap. xxiii.:

"We, however, (just as we have received), only on the Lord's day of the resurrection ought to guard, not only against kneeling, but every posture and office of solicitude; deferring even our business, lest we give any place to the devil. Similarly, too, in the period of Pentecost; which period we distinguish by the same solemnity of exultation."

Next he quotes Tertullian on Idolatry, Chap. xiv.:

"O, better fidelity of the nations to their own sects, which claims no solemnity of the Christians for itself. Not the Lord's day, not Pentecost, even if they had known them, would they have shared with us; for they would fear lest they should seem to be Christians. We are not apprehensive lest we should seem to be heathens. If any indulgence is to be granted to the flesh, you have it. I will not say your own days, but more too; for the heathens each festive day occurs but once annually; you have a festive day every eighth day."

Mr. A. then concedes that this festive eighth day was the Lord's day just mentioned. Then he quotes again, this time from Tertullian's *Ad Nationes*, Book I., Chap. xiii. :

"As often as the anniversary comes around, we make offerings for the dead as birth-day honors. We count fasting or kneeling on the Lord's day to be unlawful. We rejoice in the same privilege also from Easter to Whitsunday. We feel pained should any wine or bread, even though our own, be cast upon the ground. At every forward step and movement, at every going in and out, when we put on our clothes and shoes, when we bathe, when we sit at table, when we light the lamps, on couch, on seat, in all the ordinary actions of daily life, we trace upon the forehead the sign (of the cross)."

He closes his quotations from Tertullian by one from *De Corona*, sections 3, 4 :

"If for these and other such rules you insist upon having positive Scripture injunction, you will find none. Tradition will be held forth to you as the originator of them, custom as their strengthener, and faith as their observer. That reason will support tradition, and custom and faith, you will either yourself perceive, or learn from some one who has."

Now while Mr. A. cites the references to these garbled extracts, he does so by the use of a foot note, indicated by employing figures. And he is probably correct in supposing that not more than one out of a hundred will notice that his last quotation has nothing to do in any way with the subject of the Lord's day. There is not a word in the connection from which it is taken on that topic. He has made four quotations from four different works of that author, on four different subjects, and has thrown them together and then remarked upon them as if they were so much testimony given respecting the Lord's day, or first day of the week. And all to show that Tertullian did not regard the Lord's day of any direct divine authority.

Suppose that I could find some one saying that the early Christians kept the seventh day of the week, as did the Jews, and regarded themselves as under the law which required its observance, and then I find some other work of that same author, speaking of some things which they have come to practice by tradition and not by direct Scripture command, which he says we *don't claim divine authority for these things*, and then argue that my authority confessed that what they did was simply from custom. would not every man regard me as a falsifier of history? I would be making the writer say that he had no authority for the Sabbath when he was not talking on the subject in any way. And yet that is just what Mr. A. does for Tertullian. He says, too, that he has given all that Tertullian has said on the subject of the Lord's day but one mere reference. Well, this is what Tertullian says in so many words:

"The Lord's day is the holy day of the Christian Church. We have nothing to do with the Sabbath. The Lord's day is the Christian's solemnity."

It is no pleasure to expose the tricks of unworthy men. I am ashamed that any man can be found claiming to be a believer in Christ with no higher motive before him. He suppresses the testimony of the men from whom he pretends to quote; applies words written on one subject to another topic, and then draws conclusions that are not even warranted by his patched deliverances. I will, with this brief notice, dismiss Mr. Andrews, believing him to be unworthy of the confidence of any reader.

Let us now hear from Justin Martyr, in his Apology to Antoninus, page 67, A. D. 140. This man had been raised in Palestine, and only writes a little on this side of the apostle John. He says:

"On the day called Sunday all who live in cities, or in the country, gather in one place, and the memoirs of the apostles or the writings of the prophets are read, as long as time permits, then the president verbally instructs and exhorts to the imitation of these good things. Then we all rise together and pray; then bread and wine and water are brought and the president offers prayers and thanksgiving according to his ability, and the people say, amen. There is a distribution to each, and a partaking of that over which thanks have been given, and a portion is sent by the deacons to those who are absent. The wealthy among us help the needy; each gives what he thinks fit; and what is collected is laid aside by the president who relieves the orphans and the widows, and those who are sick or in want from any cause, those who are in bonds, and strangers sojourning among us; in a word, he takes care of all who are in need. We meet on Sunday because it is the first day, when God created the world, and Jesus Christ rose from the dead."

We have already seen that Sunday was a common term by which to speak of the first day of the week, or Lord's day. Tertullian and some others call it the "eighth day," that is, the next day after the seventh. The reason that Justin here prefers the "Sunday" to any other, is that he would be understood by the Emperor to whom he addressed the Apology, in so doing, whereas if he employed the term Lord's day, he would fail of his purpose.

The language of Pliny, the Governor of Bithynia, to the Emperor Trajan, reveals this same custom. I quote from Blackburn's History, p. p. 25, 26 : "And this was the account which they gave of the nature of the religion they once professed, whether it deserve the name of crime or error: That they were accustomed to meet on a stated day, before sunrise, and repeat among themselves a hymn to Christ as to a God, and to bind themselves as with an oath not to commit any wickedness, nor to be guilty of theft, robbery, or adultery, never to deny a promise or break a pledge; after which it was their custom to separate, and to meet again at a promiscuous, harmless meal (doubtless the love feast connected with the Lord's Supper)."

Our author thinks that this letter of Pliny was written about the year 112. Most historical critics put it several years sooner. At any rate it was but a few years after the death of the apostle John. And as we have the united testimony of history and Scripture that the disciples did observe the first day of the week, Sunday or Lord's day, as they at any time chose to call it, this is beyond any reasonable question, the meaning of this *stated day*, on which they met for the purpose of breaking bread.

I will now close the historical discussion of this question. We have seen that many of the best authorities state as plainly as they can, that the early Christians met on the first day of the week and give their reasons for doing so, that it was the day on which the Lord rose from the dead, and, on that day, the apostles and those Christians taught by them, met to break bread and drink wine, in memory of the bruised body and shed blood of the Lord Jesus. We have seen, too, that at an early time there were Judaizing teachers trying to bring the disciples back again under bondage to the law of Moses. That some of these were determined that they would keep the Sabbath, although they did not refuse to observe the first day of the week as a sacred day, made so by the resurrection of the Lord Jesus. Hence there were some who kept both days. But history is as clear as it can be that, as they came to understand the nature of the Gospel of Christ, they discontinued their devotions to the law, as such. And against this, there is no opposing testimony. History cannot be tortured into the support of the seventh day of the week. The most that the Advent historian has tried to do was to cast some doubt on keeping the Lord's day. And we have seen that even this cannot be done, only as history is falsified, and made to depose upon subjects and speak language that the writers themselves never thought of.

Usually when history is made to speak on the subject, the advocate of seventh-day-ism says: "Well, there is nothing in it any way." Now, as we said in the beginning of this part of our investigation, we do not regard it as an end to the controversy, but that it is a testimony, to the extent of the candor and critical ability of the whole church. Nay, more, they quit the Sabbath and began to keep the Lord's day, and for this, there could have been no inducement or producing cause, but the honest conviction that they were not under the law, but were only to follow Christ and the apostles. And with the exception of a few Judaizers here and there, who have not even been able to make spots in history, there has never been any doubt on the correctness of observing the first day of the week.

CHAPTER V.

THE TEACHING OF THE SCRIPTURES RESPECTING THE DAY ON WHICH CHRISTIANS SHOULD MEET FOR WORSHIP.

The Scriptures are the only infallible rule of faith and practice. Just to the extent that they teach us on this subject we will feel warranted in asking that the practice of the whole church shall agree. We know that the early Christians did not keep the Sabbath. We know that the apostles taught them that they were free from the law by the body of Christ, and hence that no one should be permitted to judge them in meat or drink, or in respect of a new moon or of a Sabbath. We know, too, that the early Christians understood that they were free from the law, and that they did not keep the seventh day, except a few Judaizing persons, who also kept Lord's day. But the question which now remains is what day should we keep? or should we keep any? Now, let it be said in fairness that the Scriptures are not very abundant on this subject. Happily, however, we are dealing now with believers, who will be satisfied with one full statement of command from Christ or any one of the apostles, or any clear and certain practice. Those to whom we now appeal do not suppose that a great number of statements are necessary to make the Word of God true.

I. The first fact that seems to govern in the matter, in the primitive church, was the resurrection of Christ on the first day of the week. Let me cite a few verses in the 24th chapter of Luke, which I think will be sufficient to prove that it was on the first day of the week that Jesus rose from the dead :

"Now upon the first *day* of the week, very early in the morning, they came unto the sepulchre, bringing the spices which they had prepared, and certain *others* with them. And they found the stone rolled away from the sepulchre. * * * And he said unto them, What manner of communications *are* these that ye have one to another, as ye walk, and are sad? And the one of them, whose name was Cleopas, answering said unto him, Art thou only a stranger in Jerusalem, and hast not known the things which are come to pass in these days? And he said unto them, What things? And they said unto him, Concerning Jesus of Nazareth, which was a prophet mighty in deed and word before God and all the people: And how the chief priests and our rulers delivered him to be condemned to death, and have crucified him. But we trusted that it had been he which should have redeemed Israel: And beside all this, to-day is the third day since these things were done. Yea, and certain women also of our company made us astonished, which were early at the sepulchre; And when they found not his body, they came, saying, that they had also seen a vision of angels, which said that he was alive."

There can be no doubt in the mind of any one who believes this account to be correct, that Jesus rose from the dead on the first day of the week. This event is of the greatest importance. It was his victory over death that was to be celebrated to the end of time. It was great to speak a world from naught, but it was greater to redeem. And no event so concerned the race as the resurrection; overcoming the unseen; conquering the last enemy. Israel had been commanded to keep the Sabbath because they had been delivered from the bondage of Egyptian slavery, but while their Sabbath was a fitting rest from the toils and hardships of the merciless lash of the taskmaster, the Christian's first day is a fitting symbol of that new life and new joy which we have in Christ; and while their Passover might tell surely enough of that mercy which had spared them while God administered justice to Egypt, the Lamb slain from the foundation of the earth, seen in the Lord's supper, is the chosen mark of the purchase price which redeems from sin and death.

It would seem most unreasonable that we, having come to the Antitype should now return to the shadow.

Jesus appeared to His disciples several times that day in a way to enlighten them upon the subject of the purpose had in view in his coming into the world. He showed himself to them by many infallible proofs, to Mary, to other women, to Peter, to two disciples as they walked into the country, and then again to the ten as they sat at meat that evening. And at last He opened their minds that they might understand the Scriptures, as He rehearsed to them what was said of Him in the Law and in the Prophets and in the Psalms.

II. Christ met especially with His apostles on the first day of the week. See John 20: 19-29.

"Then the same day at evening, being the first *day* of the week, when the doors were shut where the disciples were assembled for fear of the Jews, came Jesus and stood in the midst, and saith unto them, Peace *be* unto you. And when He had so said, he shewed unto them *His* hands and His side. Then were the disciples glad, when they saw the Lord. Then said Jesus to them again, Peace *be* unto you: as *my* Father hath sent me, even so send I you. And when he had said this, he breathed on *them*, and saith unto them, Receive ye the Holy Ghost: Whosesoever sins ye remit, they are remitted unto them; *and* whosesoever *sins* ye retain, they are retained. But Thomas, one of the twelve, called Didymus, was not with them when Jesus came. The other disciples therefore said unto him, We have seen the Lord. But he said unto them, Except I shall see in His hands the print of the nails, and put my finger into the print of the nails, and thrust my hand into his side, I will not believe. And after eight days again his disciples were within, and Thomas with them: *then* came Jesus, the doors being shut, and stood in the midst, and said, Peace *be* unto you. Then saith He to Thomas, Reach hither thy finger, and behold my hands; and reach hither thy hand, and thrust *it* into my side; and be not faithless, but believing. And Thomas answered and said unto him, My Lord and my God. Jesus saith unto him, Thomas, because thou hast seen me, thou hast believed: blessed *are* they that have not seen, and *yet* have believed."

The first meeting of the Master with His apostles must have been of the most joyous character. His breathing on them, and promising to them the Holy Spirit; the commission which He gave them must have inspired them with new thoughts and purposes. The recollections of the occasion would never depart from them during their lives; and they would fill the first day of the week with sacred and holy thought. They could not fail to see in it connections with the new life in Christ.

It seems, too, that the Master was intending to impress this thought and feeling on their hearts by appearing to them in a remarkable way on the next first day.

But when we speak of Jesus appearing to the disciples "after eight days," and yet on the first day of the week, our Advent friends make quite a stir about our assumption. They claim that the language can not mean less than an intervention of eight days, and that this second meeting was therefore near the middle of the week.

It seems as nothing to them for us to say that the critics in all ages of the church have regarded it as equal to saying, that on the next first day of the week, Thomas being with them, Jesus came, etc., for the literal interpretation, according to our way of computing time, will suit their theory better. I will quote Dr. Barnes on this passage, as a sample of the whole number of commentators. He says:

"*And after eight days again*—that is, on the return of the first day of the week. From this it appears that they thus early set apart this day for assembling together, and Jesus countenanced it by appearing twice with them. It was natural that the apostles should observe this day, but not probable that they would do it without the sanction of the Lord Jesus. His repeated presence gave such a sanction, and the historical fact is indisputable that from this time this day was observed as the Christian Sabbath. See Acts 20 : 7; 1 Cor. 16 : 2; Rev. 1 : 10."

From this decision I know of no author of note who dissents. One would naturally suppose that they have had some reasons for this unanimity of opinion. But as our Sabbatarian friends are not willing to grant that these men have had any reason for their conclusions, except the necessity of finding authority for an unscriptural service, it seems proper and right that we should turn aside for a moment and ask upon what authority they all suppose that "after eight days" means on the next first day of the week.

It seems to be known to every one except Sabbatarians that the ancients were accurate in the use of ordinals—first, second, third, etc.—but in the use of the cardinals—one, two, three, etc.—they were quite inaccurate, as we decide accuracy. It is on account of this looseness of speech that Matt. 17 : 1—"six days after"—is equal only to about "eight days after"—Luke 9: 26.

Compare a few passages on the resurrection of Christ and it will be clear that the cardinal eight days after is the eighth day, put in ordinals. In John 2 : 19: "Destroy this temple, and after three days I will raise it up again." With Adventist count this would require three full days to intervene, counting the day of crucifixion one, and the day of rising would be the fifth. And yet in Matt. 27:67 the promise was made that He would rise again on the third day. Hence their cardinal "after three days" was exactly equal to their ordinal, "on the third day." Compare Mark 8:31 with Matt. 16:21, and we have these two ways of computing time fairly contrasted. According to Mark, Jesus said "after three days," but according to Matthew he said, "on the third day." Now the only way these statements can be reconciled is by acknowledging the different modes of counting time. That these were the exact equal of each other, no man who believes the records dares to deny. And yet according to Advent calculation they would differ two days. "After three days" would place three whole days between the death and the resurrection of the Savior; "on the third day" makes the number two less. According to 1 Kings 12:5-12, we read:

"And he said unto them, Depart yet *for* three days, then come again to me. And the people departed. And king Rehoboam consulted with the old men that stood before Solomon his father while he yet lived, and said, How do ye advise that I may answer this people? And they spake unto him, saying, If thou wilt be a servant unto this people this day, and wilt serve them, and answer them, and speak good words to them, then they will be thy servants forever. But he forsook the counsel of the old men, which they had given him, and consulted with the young men that had grown up with him, *and* which stood before him: and he said unto them, What counsel give ye that we may answer this people, who have spoken to me, saying, Make the yoke which thy father did put upon us lighter? And the young men that were grown up with him spake unto him, saying, Thus shalt thou speak unto this people that spake unto thee, saying, Thy father made our yoke heavy, but make thou it lighter unto us; thus shalt thou say unto them, My little finger shall be thicker than my father's loins. And now whereas my father did lade you with a heavy yoke, I will add to your yoke: my father hath chastised you with whips, but I will chastise you with scorpions. So Jeroboam and all the people came to Rehoboam the third day, as the king had appointed, saying, Come to me again the third day."

Here again it is seen that "after three days" means the same in their style of computation as "on the third day." And in Esther 4 : 15; 5 : 1, the same manner is preserved :

"Then Esther bade them return Mordecai this answer, Go, gather together all the Jews that are present in Shushan, and fast ye for me, and neither eat nor drink three days, night or day : I also and my maidens will fast likewise; and so will I go in unto the king, which is not according to the law; and if I perish, I perish. Now it came to pass on the third day, that Esther put on her royal apparel, and stood in the inner court of the king's house, over against the king's house: and the king sat upon his royal throne in the royal house, over against the gate of the house."

Matt. 27 : 62-64 is a case in hand :

"Now the next day, that followed the day of the preparation, the chief priests and Pharisees came together unto Pilate, saying, Sir, we remember that that deceiver said, while he was yet alive, After three days I will rise again. Command therefore that the sepulchre be made sure until the third day, lest his disciples come by night, and steal him away, and say unto the people, He is risen from the dead : so the last error shall be worse than the first."

Now by every rule known to hermeneutics we are compelled to say that in their manner the cardinal "after three days," or "after eight days," was only equal to their ordinal "on the third day," or "on the eighth day." Hence it is that all the critics have regarded the language of John to mean on the eighth day after, which could mean nothing else than on the next first day.

This, too, accounts for Tertullian making use of the eighth day for the resurrection day. This language was common also to many others.

III. *The Holy Spirit came, to remain on the earth, on the first day of the week.*

For the present we take it for granted that the day of Pentecost was the first day, for we will argue that point in another and more proper place.

Jesus had promised them a new Helper or Comforter, one that would remain with them forever, who would guide them into all truth, who would receive the things of Christ and deliver them to the apostles, and bring all things to their memories that he had taught them. This was the meaning of His command to them to tarry in Jerusalem till they were *endued with power* from on high. This is not to say that no mortal had ever received the Spirit before that in any way, though it was said (John 7: 39) that the Holy Spirit was not yet given. It must mean therefore that He had not been given in the way and for the purpose contained in the promise of Jesus to His apostles. On the day of Pentecost they were baptized in that Spirit—put entirely under His control. Joel had seen this event in connection with those appointments by which the world should be furnished with the light of God that bringeth salvation to all men. (See Joel 2: 28, 29.) This day was regarded by the apostles as their beginning of the new system of religion in Christ. Peter, after he had been to the house of Cornelius, defended himself for going in unto one who was uncircumcised, and especially for admitting them to gospel privileges. His appeal was to the baptism of the Spirit, which he says was like that which had been granted to the Jewish brethren "at the beginning." We know then that they regarded this new state of things, witnessed by the presence and power of the Holy Spirit, as beginning on the Pentecost, which we shall see was on the first day of the week.

This leads us to notice that it was on this occasion that the new law went forth. A law had been given from Sinai, which had served as a schoolmaster, in preparing the people for the acceptance of Christ that they might be justified by faith. But all through the period of Israelitish prophets they were being informed that there was a coming One, who should establish His throne with justice and judgment, in whom the Gentiles would trust, and for whose law the isles of the sea should wait; whose right it should be to rule, who would overturn and overturn till all things should be put under his authority. The very time, place and circumstances of the going forth of this new law was seen by the prophets.

In Isaiah 2: 1-5, we have an inspired view of this topic:

"The word that Isaiah the son of Amoz saw concerning Judah

and Jerusalem. And it shall come to pass in the last days, *that* the mountain of the Lord's house shall be established in the top of the mountains, and shall be exalted above the hills; and all nations shall flow unto it. And many people shall go and say, Come ye, and let us go up to the mountain of the Lord, to the house of the God of Jacob; and he will teach us of his ways, and we will walk in his paths: for out of Zion shall go forth the law, and the word of the Lord from Jerusalem. And he shall judge from among the nations, and shall rebuke many people; and they shall beat their swords into plow-shares, and their spears into pruning-hooks: nation shall not lift up sword against nation, neither shall they learn war any more. O house of Jacob, come ye, and let us walk in the light of the Lord."

To the same effect, and in almost the same language, is the statement made by the prophet Micah, 4:1, 2:

"But in the last days it shall come to pass, *that* the mountains of the house of the Lord shall be established in the top of the mountains, and it shall be exalted above the hills; and people shall flow unto it. And many nations shall come, and say, Come, and let us go up to the mountain of the Lord, and to the house of the God of Jacob; and he will teach us of his ways, and we will walk in his paths: for the law shall go forth of Zion, and the word of the Lord from Jerusalem."

Let us note a few facts in these prophetic statements:

1. That this law should go forth from Zion and Jerusalem, or from Mt. Zion in Jerusalem.
2. That the law should be first presented to the descendants of Jacob.
3. That it would go forth in the last days of Judah, as a people, and Jerusalem (as a city of the Jews), or shortly before the ruin of that people.
4. At the time of this law going forth all nations should be represented.
5. These peoples shall have flown to Jerusalem to hear the word of the Lord.
6. The effect of this law will be to make peace, to subdue the brutal passions of men, and cause wars to cease.

Now, as we know that the law of Christ is the last revelation of God to the race, it follows that it was his law which was referred to.

It was offered first to the seed of Israel; it went forth from Zion; it was shortly before the fall of Jerusalem and the dispersion of the Jewish people, and all nations were present (by representatives) at that time. (See Acts 2: 5). The gospel, the law of Christ, which went forth on that occasion, is the law of peace; its justice and mercy will remove cruelty and bloodshed. Indeed, every feature of these predictions has its fulfillment in the occasion of the Pentecost.

Not only so, but the comment of the Master on these Scriptures fixes their meaning beyond a peradventure. See Luke 24: 44-49:

"And he said unto them, These are the words that I spake unto you, while I was yet with you, that all things must be fulfilled, which were written in the law of Moses, and in the prophets, and in the psalms, concerning me. Then opened he their understanding, that they might understand the Scriptures, and said unto them, Thus it is written, and thus it behooved Christ to suffer, and to rise from the dead the third day: and that repentance and remission of sins should be preached in his name among all nations, beginning at Jerusalem. And ye are witnesses of these things. And, behold, I send the promise of my Father upon you: but tarry ye in the city of Jerusalem, until ye be endued with power from on high."

When we search for the "thus it is written" for the conditions of pardon being preached *among all nations, beginning at Jerusalem*, we are taken right back to the Scriptures which I have quoted from Isaiah and Micah. Hence we have the comment of Jesus respecting those prophecies.

This enduement for which they were to wait had been promised by the prophet Joel (2. 28, 29), and reiterated by the Master (John 14: 15, 16, 26; 15 · 26; 16: 7-14). All these promises were fulfilled on the Pentecost. Acts 2: 3, 4, 14-18:

"And there appeared unto them cloven tongues like as of fire, and it sat upon each of them. And they were all filled with the Holy Ghost, and began to speak with other tongues, as the Spirit gave them utterance. . . . But Peter, standing up with the eleven, lifted up his voice, and said unto them, Ye men of Judea, and all ye that dwell at Jerusalem, be this known unto you, and hearken to my words: for these are not drunken, as ye suppose, seeing it is but the third hour of the day. But this is that which was spoken by the prophet Joel, And it shall come to pass in the last days, saith God, I will pour out of my Spirit upon all flesh: and your sons and your daughters shall prophesy, and your young men shall see visions, and your old men shall dream dreams: and on my servants, and on my handmaidens, I will pour out in those days of my Spirit; and they shall prophesy."

Now, when an inspired apostle says, "*This is* that which was spoken of," etc., it is not safe to say it was *not*. Hence we are bound to see in the events of the Pentecost the fulfillment of Joel's prediction, or deny the inspiration of Peter.

And that they understood this also to be the fulfillment of the promise of the Lord to them, there can be no doubt. They now act under the commission in preaching repentance and remissions of sins to the people. And afterward, when like demonstration attended him at the house of Cornelius (Acts 10: 44-48; 11: 15-18), both Peter and the other apostles understood it to mean that to the Gentiles were granted repentance to life. This question was settled by showing that the same manifestation was there which attended them "*at the beginning.*"

There is, therefore, no other conclusion possible, but that the first Pentecost after the ascension of Jesus was the time of the beginning of the gospel being preached in its facts. See 1 Cor. 15: 1-4.

This event was never lost sight of by the apostles and early Christians. The new law of the newly coronated King now goes forth. Hence it is the birth-day of the kingdom of Christ, the Church of Christ on earth.

Jesus had said, "On this Rock I *will* build my church," and now, the foundation having been laid, the structure begins to rise, constituted of lively stones, built up an spiritual house, as God's dwelling place upon the earth.

But some one denies, perhaps, that the Pentecost came on the first day of the week. To this let us devote a little attention. The institution of the Pentecost, or the feast of weeks, shows that it always occurred on the first day of the week. See Lev. 23: 15: 21:

"And ye shall count unto you from the morrow after the

sabbath, from the day that ye brought the sheaf of the wave-offering; seven sabbaths shall be complete: even unto the morrow after the seventh sabbath shall ye number fifty days; and ye shall offer a new meat-offering unto the LORD. Ye shall bring out of your habitations two wave-loaves of two tenth-deals: they shall be of fine flour, they shall be baken with leaven, they are the first-fruits unto the LORD. And ye shall offer with the bread seven lambs without blemish of the first year, and one young bullock, and two rams: they shall be for a burnt-offering unto the LORD, with their meat-offering, and their drink-offerings, even an offering made by fire of sweet savour unto the LORD. Then ye shall sacrifice one kid of the goats for a sin-offering, and two lambs of the first year for a sacrifice of peace-offerings. And the priest shall wave them with the bread of the first-fruits for a wave-offering before the LORD, with the two lambs: they shall be holy to the LORD for the priest. And ye shall proclaim on the self-same day, that it may be an holy convocation unto you: ye shall do no servile work therein. It shall be a statute forever in all your dwellings throughout your generations."

The meaning of Pentecost is *fiftieth*, and having numbered seven Sabbaths, the day following, the fiftieth, would be the Pentecost, as seen in the sixteenth verse. Hence the giving of the law of Christ, the beginning of the gospel, the descent of the Spirit, the birth of the reign of Christ on the earth, came on the first day of the week.

Indeed, the law from Mt. Sinai seems to have been given on the first day of the week. Compare Ex. 12:18; 19:1, 14-16, and the following facts appear: the lamb was killed on the 14th of the first month; it was on the third day of the third month that the law was given. "The self-same day" does not mean the day of the month on which Israel started from Egypt, for there is no reference to that event. It means the first day of the month. Add two to this, then thirty for the previous month, then seventeen for the first month (for only thirteen are to be subtracted, seeing that the lamb was slain on the 14th), and you have the law given on the fiftieth, which, in itself, seems to be the origin of the Pentecost.

CHAPTER VI.

HOW THE APOSTLES UNDERSTOOD THE SUBJECT OF THE LORD'S DAY.

We have seen already that they did not regard themselves under the law, and that they did not keep the Sabbath; that there is no case on record where a company of Christians only met together on the Sabbath day for any purpose. And yet it is probable that those Judaizing teachers who came down to Antioch, and taught that they must be circumcised and keep the law, or they could not be saved, kept the Sabbath. But if it had been regarded as binding on Christians, we should have had at least some account of its observance somewhere. We have seen, too, that the apostles taught the disciples that they were free from the law, and that no man had any right to judge them in respect of the Sabbath. We have seen, too, that the Christian world has been a unit on the subject of the observance of the Lord's day, or first day of the week. We have also seen many reasons why they should have reached this conclusion, but we now come to examine more closely into what the apostles have said concerning this matter, directly.

From Hebrews 10:25, we learn that they had a regular day or time of meeting together, for it is inconceivable that they should be exhorted to not neglect the assembling of themselves together. if there was no appointed time for such a gathering. No one could be blamed for not being present, if there was no understanding as to the time and place of meeting. We learn, a little on this side of the apostles, that they had a stated time, namely, on Sunday—the resurrection day—when they met everywhere. in the villages and in the country localities, where they could do so without being persecuted, and where they could do no better they met in caves and fastnesses of the mountains.

But the question which now engages our attention is, What have the apostles said directly on the subject of keeping the Lord's day, or first day of the week? This brings us to our argument number

IV. *The primitive church met together on the first day of the week to break bread. This is the direct statement of Acts XX: 7.*

A number of things are said in answer to this, such as that such language does not declare a practice, but simply records an occurrence. Once in the history of Christian work it happened that they met on the first day of the week to break bread, and that is nothing more than an incident.

And yet, if Sabbatarians could find somewhere in the New Testament, a gathering of Christians for Christian worship, only, on the seventh day, it would be regarded as a custom, and therefore a guide to Christians at the present time.

They try to tell us that there is no evidence that Paul regarded the day as sacred, from the fact that he went on his journey the next morning, which, according to their count, was still the first day of the week. Let us read the connection, beginning with the fourth and closing with the eleventh verse:

"And there accompanied him into Asia, Sopater of Berea; and of the Thessalonians, Aristarchus and Secundus, and Gaius of Derbe, and Timotheus; and of Asia Tychicus and Trophimus. These going before, tarried for us at Troas. And we sailed away from Philippi, after the days of unleavened bread, and came unto them to Troas in five days; where we abode seven days. And upon the first *day* of the week, when the disciples came together to break bread, Paul preached unto them, (ready to depart on the morrow) and continued his speech until midnight. And there were many lights in the upper chamber, where they were gathered together. And there sat in a window a certain young man named Eutycus, being fallen into a deep sleep; and as Paul was long preaching, he sunk down with sleep, and fell down from the third loft, and was taken up dead. And Paul went down, and fell on him, and embracing *him* said, Trouble not yourselves; for his life is in him. When he therefore was come up again, and had broken bread, and eaten, and talked a long while, even till break of day, so he departed."

Now from this we learn, (1) That they remained there at Troas seven days, and therefore passed a Sabbath in that place. Hence, if there was any such observance as Sabbatarians contend for, it is unaccountable that no mention is made of it. (2) The purpose of the Lord's day meeting will account for their remaining there the seven days. We have no other custom which will indicate any sufficient reasons for this delay. (3) "When the disciples were met together to break bread" is the manner of recording a custom, not a mere occurrence. Hence, to read the passage simply to find its contents, leaves the conviction on all minds, as we have seen before, that they met for the purpose of breaking bread, and that he might enjoy that communion with them. Paul had remained that length of time with them.

But it is said that Paul went on his journey on that day; not only so, but he went on foot, across the country. They forget that there is no reference to his stopping any time during his whole ministry for the Sabbath, and that their argument would ruin their doctrine of the Sabbath. Paul was in haste to reach Jerusalem by the Pentecost, and if he should have gone forward on that day rather than to take his chances of finding another opportunity to cross the waters, there would be nothing strange about it. Still, they have to assume that the first day of the week, on which they met together to break bread, and the "morrow," on which he was ready to depart, were the same day. In the second place, they assume that the journey spoken of in the thirteenth verse was on the first day of the week. It is not so stated; neither is it a necessary inference. And in the third place there would be nothing in it, if they should be able, under the circumstances, to find Paul going on his way. What we do know is that the disciples met together to break bread, and that this was the purpose for which they met. It was therefore to them a day of sacred devotion in the service of the Lord.

V. Paul's directing the saints in their worship on the first day of the week, both in Corinth and the churches in Galatia, shows that the day was everywhere so employed. See 1 Corinthians 16: 1, 2.

It is sometimes said that this language does not indicate that the first day of the week was regarded as a sacred day, for it was to be devoted to secular purposes; they were to make it a day of money raising, or for the laying apart of some of their income for the purpose of sending a present to the saints who were in Judea.

We find that all bodies of Christians do, and ever have, provided on this day for the temporal necessities of those for whom they are responsible. If they have not done this wholly on the first day of the week, they have at least largely accomplished that work on that day. Can we prove in that way or by that fact that they have not regarded the day as sacred? To ask the question is enough. Every man who will stop long enough to think, will acknowledge that their providing for this benevolence can in no way interfere with the idea that they regarded the day as sacred. Indeed it strengthens that thought. To make such provisions for the needy, would be as religious an act as could be performed on that or any other day.

Again, it is said that there is no evidence that they met together at all on the first day of the week; that the only direction in the matter is that of laying by in store such an amount of their earnings as they would be able to spare.

But the very purpose had in view in this request would be defeated in that way. Paul thought he might be in great haste, and there would be no time for such gathering of means after his arrival, and therefore he would have it all provided in a place where it might be used at once; that if he should reach the city in the evening and wish to depart in the morning, the contribution would be ready, and that no time would be lost. But if this money should be at their homes, the collection would yet have to be made. But why request them to lay by them in store on the first day of the week? Why not **say** to them, Lay up all you can till I come, so that the amount which I ought to take will be provided for? It is not too much to say that such would have been his directions in the matter if such had been his thought.

It is strange again, if they are correct in this view, that the whole Christian world differs with them in reference to it. Almost everywhere it is cited as a rule for raising the necessary expenses of church and missionary work.

The rendering of this passage by Benjamin Wilson in the Emphatic Diaglott brings out the meaning more clearly than that of the Common Version:

"And concerning the collection which is for the saints;—as I directed the congregation in Galatia, so also do you. Every first day of every week, let each of you lay something by itself, depositing as he may be prospered, so that when I come, collections may not then be made."

Dr. Macknight takes a like view of the passage and renders it:

"Now concerning the collection which is for the saints, as I ordered the churches of Galatia, so also do ye. On the first day of every week, let each of you lay somewhat by itself, according as he may be prospered, putting it into the treasury, that when I come, there may be then no collections."

The Doctor takes the same view of the purpose of the collection which has already been mentioned, and therefore urges that the use of a treasury or chest was employed by them for this purpose. He then says:

"From this passage it is evident that the Corinthian brethren were in use to assemble on the first day of the week for the purpose of worshiping God. And as the apostle gave the same order to the Galatians, they likewise must have held their religious assemblies on the first day of the week."

The only rational way of accounting for this order is the thought which has been generally, almost unanimously, adopted —that Paul selected the day on which the congregation met for worship, and ordered that at these regular meetings they should thus participate in the contribution. This will account for the same demand being made of the Corinthians that was made of the congregations in Galatia.

If we were looking for the one great purpose of the meeting on every Lord's day, it would be the same as that of the church at Troas—"the breaking of bread," or the communion. That this may appear to us as it was, let us turn and read 1 Cor. 11 · 20-30:

"When ye come together therefore into one place, *this* is not to eat the Lord's supper. For in eating every one taketh before *other* his own supper: and one is hungry, and another is drunken. What! have ye not houses to eat and to drink in? or despise ye the church of God, and shame them that have not? What shall I say to you? shall I praise you in this? I praise *you* not. For I have received of the Lord that which also I delivered unto you, That the Lord Jesus, the *same* night in which he was betrayed took bread: and when he had given thanks, he brake *it*, and said, Take, eat; this is my body, which is broken for you: this do in remembrance of me. After the same manner also *he took* the cup, when he had supped, saying, This cup is the new testament in my blood: this do ye, as oft as ye drink *it*, in remembrance of me. For as often as ye eat this bread, and drink this cup, ye do shew the Lord's death till he come. Wherefore whosoever shall eat this bread, and drink *this* cup of the Lord, unworthily, shall be guilty of the body and blood of the Lord. But let a man examine himself, and so let him eat of *that* bread, and drink of *that* cup. For he that eateth and drinketh unworthily, eateth and drinketh damnation to himself, not discerning the Lord's body."

The evident meaning of this severe reproof is that they should meet together for the purpose of partaking of the Lord's supper, but by their abuse of this holy appointment they were not really partaking of the supper at all. They had turned it into a kind of club dinner, or a Sunday feast, and had left the spiritual import of the beautiful, solemn service. It reveals the fact, however, that they should meet together for the purpose of breaking bread. The time of their meeting is found in the first part of the sixteenth chapter, which, as we have seen when clearly translated, was on every first day of the week.

Thus it is seen that, like the church at Troas, so the churches at Corinth and the churches in Galatia met every first day of the week to break bread. Hence these meetings furnished an opportunity for Paul's benevolent enterprise—raising money for the needy.

VI. Our sixth and last argument is founded on Rev. 1: 10: "I was in the Spirit on the Lord's day."

On this passage Smith's Dictionary of the Bible (American edition) has this to say: "It has been questioned, though not seriously till of late years, what is the meaning of the Greek phrase, *he kuriake hemera*, which occurs in one passage only of the Holy Scripture, Rev. 1: 10, and is in our English version translated 'the Lord's day.' The general consent, both of Christian antiquity and of modern divines, has referred it to the weekly festival of our Lord's resurrection, and identified it with the first day of the week, on which he rose, with the patristical 'eighth day,' or 'day which is both the first and the eighth,' in fact with the *ha tou haliou hemera, Solis Dies*, or Sunday, of every age of the church.

"But the views antagonistic to this general conduct deserve at least a passing notice. (1) Some have supposed St. John to be speaking, in the passage above referred to, of the Sabbath, because that institution is called in Isaiah 58:13, by the Almighty himself, 'My holy day.' To this it is replied, if St. John had intended to specify the Sabbath he would surely have used that word, which was by no means obsolete, or even obsolescent, at the time of his composing the book of the Revelations. And it is added that if an apostle had set the example of confounding the seventh and first days of the week, it would have been strange indeed that every ecclesiastical writer for the first five centuries should have avoided any approach to any such confusion. They do avoid it, for as *Sabbaton* is never used by them for the first day, so *kuriake* is never used by them for the seventh day."

The writer then proceeds to show that other interpretations were equally unsound, and that it must have the meaning generally agreed upon, namely, that of the first day of the week. Next the author shows us that all men have ever understood the Lord's day to refer to the day of the resurrection, or first day of the week. I have given a number of the quotations which are given here, but I will notice a few which I have not noticed before, that you may see just how the fathers understood these words. I quote Mr. Smith's use of them. See Vol. II; pages 1676-1680:

"The epistle ascribed to St. Barnabas, which though certainly not written by that Apostle, was in existence in the early part of the second century, has (c. 15) the following words: 'We celebrate the eighth day with joy, on which too Jesus rose from the dead.'"

The author then quotes Dionysius, bishop of Corinth, as using language quite as strong and clear as that which is put to the account of Barnabas. Then he quotes from Melito, bishop of Sardis, who had written a work on the Lord's day. He then says:

"The next writer who may be quoted is Ireneus, bishop of Lions, A. D. 178. He asserts that the Sabbath is abolished;

SABBATH OR LORD'S DAY?

but his evidence to the existence of the Lord's day is clear and distinct. It is spoken of in one of the best known of his fragments. Victor, bishop of Rome, Clement of Alexandria, Tertullian, Origen, Minucius Felix, Cyprian and his colleagues, Commodian, Victorinus, Peter, bishop of Alexandria. He introduces them all as holding the same views and as using the same phraseology respecting the first day of the week. 'They call it Lord's day, first day, eighth day, resurrection day, Sunday, but they never call it Sabbath.'"

The only reason why these men never speak of Christians meeting for worship on the Sabbath day—except a few Judaizers who kept both days—is because they did not meet on that day.

After Christ rose from the dead and was made both Lord and the anointed One—Acts 2.36—the word Lord constantly refers to him. Before this it was used of the Father, and afterward, when a quotation from the Old Testament was employed containing such use. But after it was known that all authority in heaven and earth had been given into his hands (Matt. 28:18, 19,) the apostles employed this term wholly of Christ.

We have already seen that Christians used the "Lord's day" of the first day of the week. We have not found, and can not find, that they ever spoke of the seventh day of the week by that phrase. No more could it refer to the Sabbath of the Decalogue, than "The Lord's Supper" of 1 Cor. 11:20 could have meant the Jewish Passover. As it meant the supper, or breaking of bread in honor of Jesus, so this day was the day of victory through his resurrection from the dead. "The Lord's day" of Rev. 1:10 not only refers to the first day of the week, but the use of it there shows that the phrase was familiar to all the saints at that time. To have employed an obscure term would have defeated his purpose entirely. No other day than this would have been regarded as worthy of such honorable distinction. It was the day of the Lord's victory over death; the day on which he appeared to his disciples by many infallible proofs; the day of the Spirit's descent; the day of the announcement of his kingdom, and the beginning of his church; the day on which remission of sins was first offered to the world in his name; the day on which his law went forth from Zion and his word from

Jerusalem; the day on which, from the very first, his disciples met to break bread, in memory of his dying love.

No wonder John "was in the Spirit on the Lord's day." While he was in exile for his devotion to Jesus; while he was maltreated by the great enemy of the race, who had put his Master to death, the return of this day would fill his heart with the thoughts of certain victory. He knew that the disciples were then everywhere remembering the Lord's death, were praying for his exile, and for the Master's intervention in his behalf.

The disciples soon learned that the first day of the week, being the Lord's day, was not their day; it was not a day for secular pursuits, or social mirth, but a day of holy joy in the solemn service of the Savior of men.

A word to the reader, and I have done. Let no man judge you in meat or in drink, or in respect of a holy day, or of the new moon, or of the Sabbath. The cross of Christ is of none effect to you, if you are justified by the law. But no flesh is justified by the law in the sight of God. We have seen that the whole law, Sabbath and all, was done away in Christ, and that we are now only under law to Christ. And we now lay down the challenge of Elijah, changed to our present subject: If Christ is our lawgiver, serve him; if Moses is our lawgiver, serve him. The mixing of the law and the gospel has been the great weakness of the church. I exhort you, therefore, to use your freedom in Christ Jesus; to stand fast, therefore, in the liberty of a Christian, and be not entangled in the yoke of bondage.

PUBLICATIONS OF

CHRISTIAN PUBLISHING CO.

913 PINE ST., ST. LOUIS, MO.

BAXTER (William). Life of Elder Walter Scott, with sketches of his fellow-laborers, William Hayden, Adamson Bentley, John Henry and others. Steel portrait. 450 pages, 12mo, cloth...$2 00

BAXTER (William). Life of Elder Knowles Shaw, the Singing Evangelist. 12mo, cloth. Steel portrait............... 1 25

BRADEN (Clark). The Problem of Problems, and its various Solutions; Or, Atheism, Darwinism, and Theism. Crown 8vo. 480 pages. Cloth... 2 00

BRADEN AND HUGHEY Debate. The Action, Design and Subjects of Baptism, and the Work of the Holy Spirit. 1 vol. 8vo. 687 pages 2 50

*****BRENTS (Dr. T. W.) The Gospel Plan of Salvation.** 12mo, cloth. 667 pages.. 2 50
Morocco, full gilt... 5 00

BEGG (William). Mnemonics; Or a System of Aids to Memory. By Elder William Begg, A. B. Part I—Its Principles Stated and Explained. Part II—The System Variously Applied, and many Proofs given of its Availability and Utility. 12mo. 240 pages... 1 50

BUTLER (Marie R.). Riverside; Or Winning a Soul. 12mo, 174 pages, cloth, illustrated..................................... 75

BUTLER (Marie R.). Grandma's Patience; Or, Mrs. James' Christmas Gift. 32mo, cloth, illustrated 40

*****BURNET (David Staats). The Christian Baptist.** Seven volumes in one. Edited by A. Campbell, and revised by D. S. Burnet. Contains 680 double-column pages. Cloth, $2 50; arabesque 3 00,

*****BURNET (David Staats). The Christian Sunday-School** LIBRARY. New edition, with new illustrations, written and published expressly for Christian Sunday-schools and Christian families. Neatly and substantially bound in cloth, with gilt back. Fifty books in forty volumes, 32mo, cloth..............12 00

*FRANKLIN (Benjamin). The Gospel Preacher. Vol. I. A Book for the People. A volume of Twenty Sermons written by Benjamin Franklin, Editor of the *American Christian Review*. 12mo, cloth... 2 00
Gospel Preacher. Vol. II. 12mo, cloth..................... 2 00

*FRANKLIN (Benjamin). Reynoldsburg Debate. An Oral Debate between Benjamin Franklin, a Disciple of Christ, and John A. Thompson, a Baptist; held in Reynoldsburg, Ohio, lasting four days. 12mo, cloth................... 1 25

GARRISON (J. H.) Heavenward Way. This popular little book of 100 pages, addressed to young Christians, with incentives and suggestions for spiritual growth, is meeting with a large sale among Christians, young and old, and hundreds have expressed themselves as greatly benefited by reading it. It should be in every Christian household. Price in cloth........ 50
Price in flexible cloth cut flush................................ 35

GOODWIN (Elijah). The Family Companion. A Book of Sermons on Various Subjects, both Doctrinal and Practical. 12mo. 476 pages. Cloth.................................... 1 50

GOODWIN (Mrs. M. M. B.) Autumn Leaves. A beautifully bound volume containing the sweet and tender poems of our talented sister, so widely and favorably known among the Disciples. Cloth 1 00
Morocco 1 50

GREEN (F. M.) The Life and Work of James Abram Garfield. A full, complete and accurate history of his eventful life, with incidents of his boyhood, the struggles of his youth, the success of his early manhood, his educational and religious work; his valor as a soldier, his career as a statesman, and an account of the tragic and mournful scenes connected with the close of his noble and eventful life. Also containing the Memorial Address of Hon. James G. Blaine. Illustrated with numerous engravings. Cloth, plain..................... 1 50
English cloth, beveled boards................................. 2 00
Half Morocco.. 2 50
Full Morocco'.. 3 00
Full Morocco, gilt edge 3 50

GRIFFITH (Prof. A. A.) Class Book of Oratory. A Complete Drill-Book for the practice of the principles of Vocal Physiology, and for acquiring the art of Elocution and Oratory, composing all the essential elements of vocal delivery and gesture, with all the late selections for public recitals, schools, colleges, the pulpit, private lessons, elocutionists, and all public readers. 12mo, cloth.. 1 50

GRIFFITH (Prof. A. A.) Climax Series. No. 1. A New Speaker for home and school, classes and private learners. It contains much new matter, and many selections not heretofore published; the "latest" and best gems, and selections Also suggestions on the principles to be applied in the delivery of written, printed or extemporaneous discourse. Quality of tone, for primary classes. The principal passions and emotions, and how to express them as they occur in reading. Paper..... 30
Boards.. 50

CATALOGUE OF CHRISTIAN PUBLISHING COMPANY.

Alexander Campbell's Works.

CAMPBELL (Alexander). **The Christian System,** in reference to the Union of Christians and a Restoration of Primitive Christianity as plead in the current Reformation. By A. Campbell. 12mo, 358 pages, cloth 1 50

CAMPBELL AND PURCELL. A Debate on the Roman Catholic Religion, held in Cincinnati, O., between Alexander Campbell and Right Rev. John B. Purcell, Bishop of Cincinnati. Taken down by reporters, and revised by the parties. 12mo, 360 pages. cloth................................. 1 50

CAMPBELL. Familiar Lectures on the Pentateuch, delivered before the morning class of Bethany College, during the sessions of 1869-70, by Alexander Campbell; also short extracts from his sermons during the same session, to which is prefixed a sketch of the life of President Campbell, with a fine steel portrait. Edited by W. T. Moore.................. 1 50

*****CAMPBELL. Living Oracles.** The New Testament translated from the Original Greek. By Drs. George Campbell, James MacKnight, and Philip Doddridge. With prefaces, various emendations, and an Appendix. By Alexander Campbell.
32mo, 336 pages, cloth 50
Large 8vo, cloth... 2 50

*****CAMPBELL. The Christian Baptist.** Edited by A. Campbell. Seven volumes in one. Revised by D. S. Burnet, with Mr. Campbell's last corrections. 8vo, 680 double-column pages. Cloth, $2 50; Arabesque........................ 3 00

CAMPBELL. Christian Baptism, with its Antecedents and Consequents. By A. Campbell. 12mo, 444 pages. Half leather.. 1 00
Full leather... 1 25

CAMPBELL. Popular Lectures and Addresses of the late Alexander Campbell. A new edition of this valuable work. The author, a scholar well read in every department of literature, presents in this volume the result of a life devoted to thought and study. He never substitutes speculation for facts, but confines himself to Religion, Nature and Society, in their truest, broadest and noblest extent. His wonderful power of reasoning, the ease with which he discusses the most recondite subjects, and the new light he throws upon whatever he touches, cannot fail to interest every reader. His debates on Infidelity, Catholicism, etc., are among the ablest ever published. 647 pp., 8vo, cloth 3 00

CAMPBELL. The Evidences of Christianity; A Debate between Robert Owen, of New Lanark, Scotland, and Alexander Campbell, containing an examination of the "Social System," and all Systems of Skepticism of ancient and modern times. Held in Cincinnati, O., in April, 1829. Complete in one volume, 12mo, 465 pages, cloth............................. 1 50

CARPENTER (Geo. T.)   Spiritualism vs. the Bible;
Or, Spiritualism Condemned and the Bible Vindicated. 108 pages, paper cover.. 50

CHALLEN (James). Koinonia; or, The Weekly Contribution. 32mo, cloth 40

CORY (N. E.)   The Polymathist. A work containing essays on Pastoral Work, Scriptural Exegesis, and Homiletics, with Briefs and Skeletons of Sermons by ministers of various religious bodies. Arranged and edited by N. E. Cory. 12mo, cloth.. 2 00

CREATH (Jacob). Autobiography of Jacob Creath, Jr. Edited by P. Donan. 12mo, 212 pages, cloth................... 1 25

CONTRADICTIONS OF ORTHODOXY; Or, the Chicago Controversy over Salvation. The answers of the various Chicago clergymen to the questions of the *Times'* interviewer concerning the mode of salvation; the most important sermons elicited by the agitation of the question, including those of Moody, Swing, Thomas, Mercer, Patton, &c., with a comparison of the whole with the Bible. It possesses the advantage of giving the views of leading men in the various denominations upon this important subject in their own words.
Paper... 25
Silk cloth, embossed sides..................................... 50

CHRISTOPHER (Fannie H.)   Duke Christopher; The Young Hero of Wirtemberg. A true Story of the Reformation. This book was prepared for the young in the belief that their minds often receive a deeper impression of some historic truth from the simple details of a single story, than from their widest knowledge of historic facts. And certainly they cannot become too familiar with that wonderful time when Christianity struggled out of darkness into light. 16mo, cloth.......... 40

CHRISTOPHER (Fannie H.)   Bartholet Milon; A sequel to Duke Christopher. 16mo, cloth..................... 40

DAVIS (Mrs. Eliza). The Story of an Earnest Life. A Woman's Adventures in Australia, and in two Voyages Around the World. With a Portrait of the writer. Perils by sea and land, romantic adventures, curious experiences, dramatic and tragic events crowd the volume. No one can read the story of her checkered life without feeling the deepest emotion. Second and corrected edition now ready. Cloth, 8vo. 570 pages....... 2 00
"It is a fascinating narrative, and as profitable as it is fascinating   A work of rare interest throughout."— *Christian Standard.*

DESTINY OF THE WICKED. A Debate between G. T. Carpenter, of the Church of Christ, and Rev. John Hughes, Universalist. A large volume of 469 pages of closely printed matter, abounding in Scripture and other quotations, and furnished with a textual index at the close, by means of which any passage used in the discussion can be readily found.
Cloth, 12mo.. 1 50

DUNGAN (D. R.) On the Rock; Or, Truth Stranger than Fiction. The Story of a struggle after the Truth as it is found in Christ. By D. R. Dungan. Ten editions of this book have been sold and the demand increases. It is the most popular book ever published by our people. 12mo, cloth 1 50
Morocco, gilt edge... 3 50

DUNGAN. Modern Phases of Skepticism. A series of lectures delivered before the students of Oskaloosa College. By D. R. Dungan. 12mo, cloth................................. 1 50

DUNGAN. Rum, Ruin and the Remedy. A thorough discussion of the Rum Curse, with unanswerable arguments for Prohibition. Every Prohibitionist and Temperance worker should have it. Highly commended by the press everywhere. 12mo, Cloth.. 1 00

DUNGAN—JAMIESON. A Debate on Spiritualism and the Bible. 8vo, paper cover................................... 25

EVANS (Rev. W. F.). Spiritualism on Trial. By Rev. W. F. Evans. Mr. Evans is one of the best debaters in the West, if not in the whole country, and is the terror of all forms of infidelity. Every preacher, every teacher, everybody that wants to keep posted on the subject should have this, the latest and most thorough refutation of modern Spiritualism. 12mo, Cloth.. 1 50

ERRETT (Isaac). Talks to Bereans. A series of eighteen Sermons, designed as a help and encouragement to that class of inquirers with whom the Scriptures are divine authority. 190 pages, 16mo, cloth... 1 00

ERRETT (Isaac). Walks About Jerusalem. A Search after the Landmarks of Primitive Christianity. 212 pages, 16mo, cloth... 1 00

EZZELL (S. R.) The Great Legacy. An argumentative and closely scriptural exhibition of the Gospel Plan of Salvation, under the similitude of a will, so presented as to meet popular objections, and remove prevailing difficulties. Cloth,.. 1 50
Arabesque 2 00

EVEREST (H. W.) The Divine Demonstration. A Text-Book of Christian Evidences. The author of this work is well known as one of the ripest scholars and acutest thinkers of the Christian Church. His mind has long been directed to the need of a work on the Evidences which would meet the new class of objections which have arisen in our times, and the present volume is the result of the study and preparation of years. It has been the aim to present solid argument in a popular form, to meet every reasonable objection, and at the same time to present an overwhelming demonstration of the divine origin of the Christian Religion. 12mo, cloth........... 1 50

FRANCES (Margaret). Rose Carleton's Reward. 12mo. Illustrated. 253 pages. Cloth........................ 1 00

HAYDEN (Amos Sutton). Early History of the Disciples in the Western Reserve, Ohio; with Biographical Sketches of the principal agents in our Religious Movement. 12mo. 476 pages. Cloth.. 2 00

HARTZEL (Jonas). The Baptismal Controversy. Its Exceeding Sinfulness. By Elder Jonas Hartzel. This is the latest work from the pen of this venerable and distinguished author, than whom few men are better fitted to write upon this vexed question. The work forms a neat volume of 337 pages, and contains as a frontispiece a well executed portrait and autograph of the author. 12mo, cloth...................... 1 50

HARTZEL. The Divinity of Christ and the Duality of Man. By Elder Jonas Hartzel. "Important themes handled in a masterly way by a close reasoner and a careful student of the word of God. "With as much Rationalism and Materialism as are now afloat, it is important that Disciples everywhere be fully armed. This book of 176 pages is an excellent helper in these controversies, and should be generally read and studied."—*Christian Standard.* Price, paper cover....... 75

HINSDALE (Pres. B. A.) The Genuineness and Authenticity of the Gospels: An Argument conducted on Historical and Critical Grounds. 276 pages, 12mo, cloth, extra. 1 25

***HINSDALE (B. A.) Ecclesiastical Tradition.** Its Origin and Early Growth; Its Place in the Churches; and its Value. Cloth.. 75

***HINSDALE (B. A.) The Jewish Christian Church.** A Monograph. Cloth.. 50

HAND (G. R.) D. B. Ray's Text-Book on Campbellism Exposed. A good book which will be read with interest by lovers of the truth. By G. R. Hand. 12mo, cloth.......... 1 00

***HARDIN (J. H.) The Sunday-School Helper.** A practical Hand-Book for all Sunday-School workers, containing suggestions on all phases of the work, which should be read and consulted by all workers, and will result in giving new impetus and arouse more earnest zeal in teaching and leading the people to Christ. Also an excellent essay on "Christian Woman's Responsibility in the Religious Education of the Young," by Mrs. O. A. Carr. 144 pages. 12mo, cloth.................... 50

***HERNDON (Dr. E. W.) Explanatory Notes on the S. S. Lessons for 1884.** The Scripture readings are given in both the Common Version and the Revision in parallel columns, so that a glance will show the difference. The Lesson Notes are clear, plain, pointed and free from useless verbiage and speculation. 12mo, cloth............................. 60

HOLY SPIRIT. Its Influence in Conversion. A debate between Rev. Asa Sleeth, of the Methodist Episcopal Church, and Elder J. W. Randall, of the Christian Church. Question: Do the Scriptures teach the Direct Influence of the Holy Spirit in Conversion? 12mo, 236 pages, cloth....................... 1 00

CATALOGUE OF CHRISTIAN PUBLISHING COMPANY.

JOHNSON (John T.) Biography of John T. Johnson. By John Rogers, of Carlisle, Ky. With steel portrait. 408 pages, 12mo, cloth.. 1 50

JOHNSON (B. W.) A Vision of the Ages. Or, Lectures on the Apocalypse: a complete view of the Book of Revelation. By Elder B. W. Johnson, editor CHRISTIAN-EVANGELIST. This work has been received with great favor as the best exposition of this wonderful prophetic book. Three editions have been called for within about a year of its appearance. 12mo, cloth.. 1 25

LAMAR. Commentary on the Gospel of Luke. Vol. 2 of New Testament Commentary. Crown, 8vo, 233 pages. Cloth.. 2 00
Sheep.. 2 50
Half calf.. 3 00

*LARD (M. E.) Commentary on Paul's Letter to the Romans. With a revised Greek text, compiled from the best recent authors, and a new translation. The author's well-known ability as a biblical scholar and critic is fully sustained in this, his life work. It has received the unqualified endorsement of the Disciples of Christ everywhere. One volume, octavo, 485 pages, cloth.. 3 00

*LIVING ORACLES. The New Testament, translated from the Greek. By Drs. George Campbell, James MacKnight, and Philip Doddridge. With Prefaces, various emendations and an Appendix. By Alexander Campbell, 32mo, 326 pages, Cloth.. 50
Large 8vo, cloth... 2 50

LUCAS (D. R.) Paul Darst; or, The Conflict Between Love and Infidelity. 16mo, cloth.................................... 1 00

LOUISVILLE DEBATE. "Christian Baptism; What is It?" L. B. Wilkes and J. Ditzler. 8vo, cloth, 708 pages..... 2 00

MATHES (J. M.) Western Preacher. By Elder J. M. Mathes. This is a valuable book, containing thirty sermons by twenty-four of our leading preachers, living and dead. Lithographic portrait of the author. 12mo, cloth.................... 2 00

MARTIN (J. L.) Voice of the Seven Thunders. By Elder J. L. Martin. A series of lectures on the Book of Revelation, by the late Elder J. L. Martin. It has received the highest commendations of the press, both religious and secular. It has been called "The Apocalyptic Key." Price.............. 1 50

McGARVEY (John W.) Commentary on the Gospels of Matthew and Mark. Vol. 1 of New Testament Commentary. Crown 8vo, 382 double-column pages. Cloth........ 2 00
Sheep.. 2 50
Half calf antique.. 3 00
Commentary on Mark. Sunday-School Edition............... 50

McGARVEY (J. W.) Commentary on Acts of the Apostles; with a revised version of the text. 12mo, cloth.... 1 50

SABBATH OR LORD'S DAY?

WHICH?

By D. R. DUNGAN,
Author of "On the Rock," "Rum, Ruin and the Remedy," Etc.

PRICE, 25 CENTS.

PUBLISHED BY
CHRISTIAN PUBLISHING CO.,
St. Louis, Mo.

An Instantaneous Success!

THE CHRISTIAN S. S. HYMNAL.

Every Piece a Gem.
No Dry and Useless Stuff.
All the Best Writers and Composers are Represented.

STYLES AND PRICES.

CHEAP POPULAR EDITION.

Boards, single copy, by mail	$ .30
" per dozen, by express	3.00
" per hundred "	25.00

FINE EDITION.

Silk cloth, red edge, single copy	.40
" " per dozen, by express	4.00
" " per hundred, "	32.00
Morocco, red edge, single copy	1.50
" gilt edge, "	2.00
" full gilt, "	3.00

WORD EDITION.

Boards, single copy, by mail	.15
" per dozen, by express	1.50
" per hundred "	10.00
Cloth, red edges, single copy, by mail	.20
" " " per dozen, by express	2.00

"A marvel of cheapness, sweetness, tenderness and pathos."—N. S. HAYNES.

"A perfect gem and I am sure our schools will hail its appearance with delight.."—L. L. CARPENTER.

"I fell in love with it at first sight. It is solid and will last for years."—R. L. MCHATTON.

"Unexcelled by any work I have ever examined."—M. P. GIVENS.

"I am proud of it, and shall urge our schools wherever I go to adopt it."—SIMPSON ELY.

"I do not see how it could be improved."—A. M HAGGARD.

"All that the most exacting could desire in a S. S. Hymnal."—R. C. BARROW.

"I am well pleased with it."—L. H. JAMIESON.

"The purest cream of all S. S. Music."—J. H. PAINTER.

"In my opinion the work meets a recognized want."—G. T. CARPENTER.

"Far better than Dr. Robinson's Spiritual Songs for the S. S."—J. B. WHITE.

"The Sunday-schools have a rich treasure in this Hymnal.—CHAS. LOUIS LOOS.

The Divine Demonstration.
A Text-Book of Christian Evidences.
BY H. W. EVEREST, LL. D.,
President of Butler University.

The author of this work is well known as one of the ripest scholars and acutest thinkers of the Christian Church. His mind has long been directed to the need of a work on the Evidences which would meet the new class of objections which have arisen in our times, and the present volume is the result of the study and preparation of years. It has been the aim to present solid argument in a popular form, to meet every reasonable objection, and at the same time to present an overwhelming demonstration of the divine origin of the Christian religion.

The author's design is to give a comprehensive, concise and logical restatement of Christian evidence—a restatement such as modern thought, both Christian and anti-Christian, seems to demand. To do this three subordinate purposes have been kept in view: *First*, To gather into one body all the arguments which have hitherto been adduced, and which have been thoroughly tested and found to be reliable. The preference in making selection of argument has not been for the new, but for the true and the convincing, from whatever source. Professors in theological schools and all Christian workers have long felt the need of such a text-book. Paley and Alexander are not adapted to present use. Nearly all modern writers have, in lectures or volumes, only developed certain arguments or lines of thought. There is a pressing need of some comprehensive treatise. *Second*, It has been the aim to combine these arguments into one, concise, compact *demonstration*. If the Christian evidences are to be invincible they must march in a solid phalanx. Presented in isolated chapters, lectures, or volumes, they lose half their force. Nor should this demonstration require a large volume; like an algebraic formula, a concise statement will bring the field of evidence before the mind at one view. *Third*, It has also been the aim to adapt the work to the class-room as well as to the general reader. Hence the analyses are complete and minute, and synopses of the argument are frequent.

The treatise is peculiar in at least two respects: The *form* of the proposition demonstrated and the *order* of the proof. It is assumed that the Proposition, the proof, and the order of the proof, have been given by the Holy Spirit. The Proposition is the one announced from heaven as such, viz.: that "Jesus is the Messiah, the Son of God." The whole argument gathers about the person, the nature, and the authority of Christ. If this Proposition is established all else will follow. Heaven has also given the proof and the order of its providential development. Hence the work is entitled, *The Divine Demonstration*. The older arguments from history and prophecy are much condensed, while the relation of Christianity to science and its adaptations to human nature and human society are more fully treated. One chapter is devoted to a classification of objections and a reply to them, but it has been the purpose to give a positive treatment rather than a negative one. The argument from prophecy is concisely but fully given. Two corollaries follow the demonstration, the Canon and Inspiration, since the authority of Christ must settle both these questions.

401 pages, 12mo cloth.. $1 50

THE TRACT.

EXTRACT FROM AN ESSAY BY ENOS CAMPBELL.

I LOOK upon the use of tracts in our missionary work as of incalculable value. A tract!—What is it? A printed page, merely! A page on which some good man or woman has spent a world of thought! The object is to gain a human soul. A tract! Verily, the most difficult of all literature to write effectually!

God's plan is to arouse the whole human family by the enunciation of the single truth: "This is my Son, the beloved, in whom I delight;" and he has added to this the single command: "Hear ye him." And when we gather close up to the Great Teacher, lo! we have the simple parable; and what is that but a tract? Flung out broadcast over the vast multitudes that hung upon his lips, and who cried out in the wild enthusiasm of their Oriental natures, "Never man spake as this man," who can estimate the power of these inimitable stories over the rough masses of human creatures around him?

The *use of the tract*, then, in the work of the saving of souls, either at home or abroad, is invaluable; nor is its agency altogether of modern date. Before the age of printing Wycliffe circulated his views by means of brief essays, which were passed from hand to hand and transcribed by those who wished to preserve them. Tyndale, also, in 1530, distributed tracts, and found them a potent influence in reaching the benighted masses around him. In 1742 John Wesley, that grand worker and mighty man of God, began the publication and distribution of tracts, and was the first to set the example of modern cheap prices sustained by large sales. In 1795 Mrs. Hannah More commenced, in Bath, the sale of what she called "Cheap Repository Tracts," of which 2,000,000 were sold the first year. The work thus commenced by individual effort has grown wonderfully, and by organized combinations has developed a work overpowering in its magnitude. "The Religious Tract Society," of London, was founded in May, 1799. In fifty years it has received and expended nearly $6,000,000. It has published, of various larger works, 5,138 volumes in 110 different languages—of which it has issued 500,000,000 copies; and the whole number of books, great and small, up to 1861, was 912,000,000 in 114 different languages. Our own beloved country is not behind in these grand works. "The American Tract Society," of New York, organized in 1825, reported in 1861 its gross receipts in money at $6,884,237. It has published 16,635,583 of larger volumes, and of tracts 219,454,676, with an aggregate number of pages of 5,882,630,598—and all this astounding work done in less than forty years.

The tract, then, and its living exponent, are potent energies in the hands of God for poor sin-troubled souls. The tract system is growing in the estimation of earth's greatest workers, and they have shown to the world:

1. The tract is the least expensive of all agencies for the good of man.

2. It is the most direct of all teachings, for it has no room for preambles, but without looking at or caring for surroundings, it goes straight to its mark, and asks the question, "Do you love Jesus?"

3. It is the most modest and unobtrusive of all messengers. It will go anywhere—stay anywhere—wait any length of time without being offended, until it is noticed. It finds its way into places where the more pretentious book could not gain admission—into the drinking saloons, the gambling hells, the theaters; into the most hideous and disgusting haunts of vice it goes without a tremor for its reputation, or a care for its safety.

4. It does not resent being blasphemed and vilified. It is used to being tossed out of doors with a growl or a curse, or trampled contemptuously in the mud. It knows it will frequently be torn into shreds and flung to the winds. In all humility and patience it renews its attack on sin, allied with multiplied thousands like itself, until at last it gains the conquest.

5. It comes to the poor man's cottage, far away from all churches, where there are no books, nor songs, nor prayers, nor holy lives, and quietly bides its time until the overworked wife and mother has time to peruse its pages; and then, bright memories of other and better days, when she heard of God in her childhood's home, come vividly before her, and, as she reads, her heart warms to the little sheet that tells of *rest* over yonder; and then she reads it to husband and children, and all feel the better for the consolation it brings.

www.ingramcontent.com/pod-product-compliance
Lightning Source LLC
Chambersburg PA
CBHW020136170426
43199CB00010B/769